T0386097

LGBTQ Leadership in Higher Education

LGBTQ
Leadership
in
Higher
Education

edited by **Raymond E. Crossman**

Johns Hopkins University Press
Baltimore

© 2022 Johns Hopkins University Press

All rights reserved. Published 2022

Printed in the United States of America on acid-free paper

9 8 7 6 5 4 3 2 1

Johns Hopkins University Press

2715 North Charles Street

Baltimore, Maryland 21218-4363

www.press.jhu.edu

Library of Congress Cataloging-in-Publication Data

Names: Crossman, Raymond E., 1964– editor.

Title: LGBTQ leadership in higher education / edited by Raymond E. Crossman.

Description: Baltimore : Johns Hopkins University Press, 2022. | Includes bibliographical
    references and index.

Identifiers: LCCN 2021048342 | ISBN 9781421444079 (hardcover) | ISBN
    9781421444086 (ebook)

Subjects: LCSH: Sexual minorities in higher education—United States. | Educational
    leadership—United States. | Universities and colleges—United States—
    Administration. | College presidents—United States. | College administrators—
    United States.

Classification: LCC LC2575 .L528 2022 | DDC 378.1/11—dc23/eng/20211109

LC record available at https://lccn.loc.gov/2021048342

A catalog record for this book is available from the British Library.

Special discounts are available for bulk purchases of this book. For more information, please
contact Special Sales at specialsales@jh.edu.

Contents

Preface

Charles R. Middleton

Stories are the handmaidens of language. When humans developed language, it soon followed that they had to have something to talk about. And among those things that generated conversation in all cultures, storytelling arose.

Historians are the professional storytellers, but there are many gifted amateurs in society and even in every family. Anyone who has been at a family holiday gathering knows that there is always one member who, after the feast, regales the table with tales of days gone by.

Stories are malleable as to purpose. They can be designed to amuse, to instruct, to answer questions such as "who am I and where did I come from?," and to record experience for posterity. Most of all, they enable us to tell our successors about why we mattered and what we were all about, both individually and collectively. It is noteworthy that the great poets of the ancient world were essentially storytellers.

Often the best storytellers are literary folks with a gift of language. Using language elegantly is part of the knack of telling a good story, which may be why historians are often expert prose writers. It's also about timing. Again, the best narrators of a good account follow Lord Macaulay's dictum to make the audience laugh, make them cry, and make them wait.

We have been waiting for the stories in this volume for a very long time and I, for one, am joyful that they have arrived.

This is a book of narrations organized around key themes in the lives and careers of a group of remarkable leaders in higher education. It is a book that just a short twenty years ago, at the turn of the new millennium, could not have been written and for the most basic of reasons: there was no one to write them.

Think about it. In the year 2000, Y2K and all that, only Theodora J. Kalikow. Nobody else. Oh, we were there, and some of us were even presidents. But using the standard of being publicly out (which is the twenty-first-century standard for membership in the organization that we "out" presidents formed in 2010), in 2000 there was only one.

These essays are fresh and engaging because they *are* fresh. They reflect experience of these presidential leaders over portions of the last 20 years. I'm sure that many others not included in these pages will see themselves in the commentaries, though the comments are explicitly not representative of the experiences and views of any particular organization or institution. But they do represent shared experience, and when I read them, I could hear many of the themes of my own story come through loud and clear.

To say that we live in remarkable times is a gross understatement. I suppose that few people in the past, whenever they lived, would ever have said that their times were boring and unremarkable. Sober historians reflecting back, of course, do provide that assessment from time to time.

Yet even the most exciting and energizing and scary times that I have experienced over the span of three-quarters of a century certainly did not, upon reflection, approach what's going on right now. Much is bad, but much is also wonderful. Including us: we're here, we're queer, we're fabulous: get used to us!

I was born toward the end of World War II. Both of my parents were sailors and thus were part of the Greatest Generation. Of those who write here, Theo and I alone can make that claim. I mention this because generational experiences put meaning to storytelling, and Theo and I aside, this is a book of the baby boomers and those in Generation X who followed them. In the overarching story line of LGBTQ people and civil rights, it is the baby boomers who have been the pioneers and the Gen Xers who have steadfastly worked to expand on their success. They blazed and continue to blaze the trails that crisscross all walks of life. They are my heroes. I salute them and am grateful to know and to have worked with so many of them over the years. These are women and men whom I would otherwise never have met and become colleagues with were it not for the power of our shared experiences and our desire to pay them forward for new generations to come.

My own story has been pretty well told, so I'm not going to delve into it here. But a couple of things are worth revealing if not for the first time, then in a new way.

First of all, I grew up in the South, specifically in south Florida in the 1950s. It was the time of Anita Bryant. My parents were people of that place and that time. We all read the *Miami Herald* daily, even my brother and I, and the news was a nightly topic of conversation at dinner.

I didn't know what gay was, but I did know that it was something that was to be avoided at all costs. On at least one unforgettable occasion, linking the odious views then prevalent on race to sexual orientation, my father explicitly said that it was worse even than being black. My thanks to Andrew Tobias for writing *The Best Little Boy in the World* and its sequel. I didn't know it at the time, but in practice I became a version of that little boy and grew into a man with all that boy's attributes. Perhaps that is why when young higher education professionals these days seek my counsel on how to develop their career, I essentially tell them, be the best little girl or the best little boy you can be. Be authentic, be reliable, work hard, learn constantly, and your career will take care of itself.

The second thing about my growing up was the slow realization that to be the best little boy you have to live a lie. That's not only unsustainable; it's inauthentic. Truth telling is scary, terrifying. But living a lie is worse; it's corrosive to your humanity and self-defeating over time. In the end, it makes it impossible for you to continue to be the best little boy or the best little girl. One of the reasons I lead my advice to others with "be authentic" is because if you are not authentic, you will ultimately fail.

The presidents and former presidents who are the authors of this book are all authentic women and men. Don't just take my word for it: read what they have to say, and when you get a chance, at some meeting or another, seek them out and chat them up. You'll be so glad you did.

The book ends with an essay that on the surface might not seem like a story, at least to some readers. Yet it is. Ralph Hexter is a classicist. He studies the ancient world, so it may seem odd that someone who knows so much about civilizations that are long gone should write a story about the future. Hexter's is an essay on some of what remains to be written in the LGBTQ leadership saga. I am sure that years hence we will find other things yet to be written about. But for now, there are many more chapters to be lived and thereafter to be reported by new storytellers. It's vital that future members of our tribe create those stories and ultimately come to share them with the next generation of leaders our society produces—and those leaders with the one after that. We all pay it forward.

So, in the end, for me this is both a book about what we have done so far and a challenge to others to continue to develop their stories and to tell them to the next generation that follows in their footsteps. To my colleagues and friends I say, "well done!"

LGBTQ Leadership in Higher Education

Introduction

Raymond E. Crossman

My installation ceremony as president of Adler University in 2003 began as most do. My name and the name of my partner were read aloud in an introduction to the university community before the start of the academic procession to the stage.* I'd wondered, when I first saw the script, whether some attendees would be taken aback by hearing "the gay thing" at the very top of the event, but I put away my internalized heterosexism and was pleased that the planners of the event never even asked me what I thought about the implications of following this convention. After the introduction, from the back of the lineup for the procession, I could hear the unmistakable sound from the audience of the "gay inhale," followed by what sounded like muffled crying. I decided to forgo discretion and stepped quickly out of line. I saw a young gay student and his partner, a few rows from the back, sharing tears of joy. I looked around and could detect signs of pride across a diversity of some of those attending. I remember wanting to better understand what was happening, thinking I had a lot to live up to, and realizing I ought to get back in line. This aspect of my appointment as president—that I was queer—mattered.

---

*The Adler Institute was founded in 1952; it became the Adler School in 1991 and Adler University in 2015.

This book is about why LGBTQ leadership matters. Fifteen currently serving or retired LGBTQ presidents and chancellors in higher education speak to why, to whom, and how it matters. We write from the perspective of our lived and specific experiences as queer presidents. We consider whether there is something distinctive about LGBTQ leadership and attempt to draw insights and principles from our stories. Is being queer a superpower for us as leaders, something we manage as part of our intersectional identities, or is it just another attribute of accomplished leaders? Across our essays, we attempt to address why LGBTQ leadership matters at this moment, and more broadly, why diversity, inclusion, and equity in leadership are important to meet today's challenges for higher education and human rights.

Gay and lesbian presidents in North American higher education are a recent phenomenon. Prior to this century, forerunners are few and not well known. Mary Emma Wooley, president of Mount Holyoke College from 1901 to 1937, is documented because her life on campus with her partner, Jeanette Marks, is described in their love letters, which have recently been curated by archivists (Haaga, Ochterski and Palme 2017). Jacquelyn A. Mattfeld, president of Barnard College from 1976 to 1980, does not receive recognition for being one of the first female administrators in top universities, or for braving sexism, heterosexism, and homophobia during her presidency. Theodora J. Kalikow, president of University of Maine Farmington from 1994 to 2012, bridges the early few examples to the era of contributors to this volume. Some of the authors of this collection know tales of closeted presidents whose histories will likely never be fully recounted. Several of us report our first realization of the existence of other LGBTQ presidents was through "gaydar," or intuition, at professional meetings.

In 2005, Charles R. "Chuck" Middleton organized what was likely the first discussion of advancement of LGBTQ professionals led by LGBTQ presidents in higher education at a professional meeting. Four LGBTQ presidents talked about our challenges and journey at a meeting that the organizers of the American Council on Education scheduled at its annual meeting at 7 a.m. on a Monday morning. A handful of enthusiastic administrators attended despite the hour. By 2007, the *Chronicle of Higher Education* wrote that the nation's colleges and universities counted three "openly" gay presidents. In the next few months, the *Chronicle* published corrections with additions mounting to 8 and then 11 (Fain 2007).

By 2010, Chuck and I decided the time was right to host a meeting of queer presidents in Chicago at Adler University and Roosevelt University. The then-24 known LGBTQ presidents were invited; 9 presidents attended the meeting in August 2010 and formed an organization called LGBTQ Presidents in Higher Education. A few months later, 7 presidents gathered at Antioch University Los Angeles, filmed an "It Gets Better" video (LGBTQ Presidents in Higher Education 2010), and composed a mission statement for the organization. We declared: "LGBTQ Presidents in Higher Education advances effective leadership in the realm of post-secondary education, supports professional development of LGBTQ leaders in that sector, and provides education and advocacy regarding LGBTQ issues within the global academy and for the public at large." Between 2011 and 2015, members organized more than 20 presentations across higher education associations for aspiring administrators about career advancement, for search firm professionals about barriers in presidential searches, and for trustees about inclusion in hiring. The first institute for leadership development of LGBTQ professionals in higher education was hosted by Adler University in 2015, followed by institutes in 2016 at Manhattan School of Music and in 2017 at Bastyr University Seattle. An exciting part of these institutes was that they culminated in participants marching in the gay pride parades of Chicago, New York City, and Seattle, respectively. In 2021, William Paterson University will have (virtually) hosted the next institute. Currently, the organization counts 101 LGBTQ presidents and chancellors in the United States and Canada—about one-third retired and two-thirds currently serving.

Today, LGBTQ presidents and chancellors reflect the US presidency in higher education—mostly white men. We worked against this reality in pulling together 15 contributors for this book, 8 of whom are women and one-quarter Black, Indigenous, or people of color. None of us is nonbinary or transgender, and at the time of this writing, we know only of nonbinary and transgender candidates in the process of interviewing for presidencies.* Most of the 15 authors are retired or serving in an encore as interim leaders or consultants. Most are baby boomers, with a few of us in the generation prior or afterward. The consequence—that our perspective may be less relevant to future queer leaders—is not lost on us and is examined in several of these essays. Some of us describe struggling with our privilege as leaders and with our participation in the heteronormative, sexist, and racist power structures of higher education, and I strongly believe that the next generation of leaders will be more advanced than we are in this regard. Importantly, this book was conceived and mostly written prior to the COVID-19 pandemic and prior to the renewed activism that followed the murders of Breonna Taylor and George Floyd. I know this book is the first in higher education on this subject, and at the same time, I believe we may be archiving in our essays a moment that is the forerunner to new, enormous, and necessary changes in the needs, awareness, and practice of leadership.

The structure for this collection of essays is a product of authors' relationships with one another and our beliefs about the value of

---

*Language about LGBTQ people is changing and will continue to change. We have decided to use the term *LGBTQ* to be inclusive, although none of the contributors to this book are transgender or nonbinary. We understand that not everyone will agree with this choice.

diverse and manifold voices. Contributors to this volume are dear colleagues and friends. Together, following many spirited conversations, we gleaned 12 topics for this book. Topics became chapters, and for each chapter, three authors wrote essays. Each chapter is a trio of voices, and our hope is that the effect is that of a "panel" to address each topic. For the final chapter, we invited one of us to speak about the future.

Every writer in this collection appreciates the rare privilege of reflecting on leadership. I'm grateful to many who made this volume possible, including Ash Senter and Liz Blondel, who supplied scholarship and support; Gary Hollander, Bill Waring, Bill Ouellette, and Ted Barzev, who provided wisdom and applause; and Greg Britton, who offered the invitation. I'm thankful to the student at my installation and the students, staff, faculty, trustees, and other colleagues who helped me realize that queer leadership matters. I'm most grateful to the authors of this volume for stepping out of line—before, during, and after their own installations—to ensure that LGBTQ and diverse leadership matters for our campuses and the world.

REFERENCES

Fain, P. September 7, 2007. "Openly Gay Presidents: 11 and Counting." *Chronicle of Higher Education.* https://www.chronicle.com/article/openly-gay-presidents-11-and-counting/.

Haaga, M, J. Ochterski, and C. Palmer. 2017. *Mary Woolley and Jeannette Marks: Life, Love, and Letters* [digital exhibition]. Mount Holyoke College Archives and Special Collections. htttps://ascdc.mtholyoke.edu/exhibits/show/wooleymarks.

LGBTQ Presidents in Higher Education. 2010. "LGBTQ Presidents in Higher Education." YouTube video, 4:30. https://www.youtube.com/watch?v=nUA5RZS4sCc.

CHAPTER 1

Identifying LGBTQ Leadership

Are there specific characteristics of LGBTQ leadership? Do we lead in a particular way because we're gay or lesbian? These are questions addressed in this chapter and across this volume. Contributors offer many different answers as to whether we operate specifically or consciously as LGBTQ leaders. The three authors in this opening chapter consider their own history, leadership development, and contemporary work, and they approach the question differently. Erika Endrijonas, president of a community college in southern California, considers it her—and our—responsibility to make our LGBTQ identity central to our leadership. Karen M. Whitney is a retired president of a rural public university who has continued in interim chancellor roles, and she describes LGBTQ leadership as a function of engaging majoritarian context. The third writer, Raymond E. Crossman, leads an urban private university, and he reports that his experience growing up queer has resulted in specific perspectives and talents that define his leadership. Contributors tackle related issues in subsequent chapters and offer a range of answers to these central questions.

Erika Endrijonas

What role should sexual orientation play in LGBTQ leaders' self-concepts, and how should it impact their approach to leadership? I am a gay president because being a president who "happens to be gay" devalues my gender, my feminism, and my sexual orientation, which are all components of my total story and personhood.

It wasn't until I attended my first meeting of the national organization LGBTQ Presidents in Higher Education that two very different viewpoints regarding identity came into focus. It was clear that the majority of male presidents and chancellors either saw themselves as "gay presidents," where their sexuality was central to their experience as leaders, or as presidents who "happen to be gay," where their sexual orientation was more marginal to that experience. I was one of four women leaders present, and it was clear that we were all "lesbian presidents."

This became especially enlightening when the group started to discuss strategies for how to get other gay leaders involved in the organization. One of the male presidents, who happens to be gay, made the suggestion that maybe the organization should consider allowing LGBTQ leaders who are not out to be members. The reaction from the four lesbians was immediate and clear: Hell, no. All four of us reacted in a visceral way, and I have since given a lot of thought to why. Perhaps it was because remaining closeted is a violation of everything we are trying to achieve with this organization. Perhaps it was because it felt like we would be rewarding the "passing" culture of decades past, with privilege accruing to those who passed successfully. Or perhaps it was because for us, being women and being lesbian are inextricably linked, sexuality and gender being not severable parts of the whole but coincident and symbiotic.

I recently taught a doctoral course on leadership, although my academic training is in the field of history. I was proud of my textbook choice because it included at least 15 different leadership styles, and I was sure that my students would use it to discover their own leadership philosophy over the course of the semester. However, I neglected to sufficiently review the chapter on gender, which,

I discovered when my students did, was horrible. It was an ahistorical treatment of gender and leadership in the workplace, and the treatment of sexual orientation's influence on leadership in this and other chapters was virtually nonexistent. Several of my students were stunned at the weakness of the book, and I tried to make up for it with lectures and supplemental material, but to no avail. What kind of self-respecting lesbian feminist leader was I if I didn't see how important this would be to the students, especially the gay students, in this class?

One might wonder why I took this so personally. Faculty make poor choices about textbooks all the time. However, it's different for me as an out LGBTQ leader. I have a higher responsibility. My students probably assumed that my LGBTQ identity would be my first consideration when choosing a textbook; certainly, it should have been a thoughtful consideration. My work as a president comes with a host of expectations, and it is often assumed that I will prioritize LGBTQ inclusion and social justice above everything else. At the same time, there is also the pressure to avoid creating a "gay agenda," not that I know what that would look like.

Occasionally, I have felt that I have been too hard on my colleagues who "happen to be gay." I was in a better position in some ways than some of them, several of whom were at very conservative institutions. After all, I was a president in a multicollege district, in Los Angeles, interacting with a board of trustees that had hired me seemingly without regard to my sexual orientation. In fact, when I was initially hired, I felt as if my sexual orientation was a non-topic. However, one night early in my tenure there, while out for drinks with my fellow presidents, the chancellor turned to me and asked me what my husband did for work. To his credit, when I said that I had a wife, he apologized for assuming, and then he did a very strange thing: He high-fived me. Being high-fived for being lesbian was one of the subtlest forms of differential treatment I have ever experienced. The lesson here is this: Even in California, even in academia, even in a group of kind, enlightened people with the best of intentions, heterocentrism persists.

In fact, there is no such thing as a person "who happens to be" anything other than a composite of their various identities because it is impossible to divorce one's identities from one's own experiences and one's own personhood. For example, I am not just a president who had her back window smashed in with a rock and her car defecated on; I am a gay president whose back window was smashed because it had a gay pride pink triangle sticker on it. I am also not just a president whose spouse came out of a bank to find her car defaced; I am a lesbian president whose spouse's car had *dyke* written all over it in lipstick. These experiences remain reminders that, while we have come a long way in 25 years, we must not grow complacent, because complacency will be dangerous for the people we serve.

If one extrapolates this dichotomy to the work we do on our campuses, thinking of myself as a president who "happens to be gay" might allow me to slide into thinking that a food-insecure student is just a student who happens to be hungry, a housing-insecure student is just a student who happens to be homeless, or that a poor student is a student who just happens to be poor. Instead, it is imperative that I remain vigilant about creating an institution that serves the whole student, and that the effort to root out the vestiges of racism, sexism, homophobia, and privilege never ends, because the work isn't done until the playing field is level.

The other imperative to considering myself a gay president rather than a president who "happens to be gay" is that I am a role model, and I never know whether there is someone in any given venue who is trying to summon the courage to come out. If I downplay my sexual orientation, which being a president who "happens to be gay" entails, what kind of message does that send? In our effort to close the equity achievement gaps among our students, we are very intentional about hiring faculty and staff that reflect our student population demographics. When students see people in faculty or leadership roles who look like them, they can see themselves achieving at a similar level. The same is true for our LGBTQ students.

It may seem unfair to put such responsibility on our shoulders as LGBTQ leaders, or to say that presidents who "happen to be gay" are less than dedicated to social justice for our students, faculty, and staff, but it is not unfair. It is wholly appropriate. We have chosen a role that matters in profound ways to real people's lives, and we must treat it as a sacred trust.

Karen M. Whitney

When I served as a university president I was very out as a lesbian. I clearly knew that my human identity, including being a lesbian, informed my approach to leadership. Some of my proudest moments as president were when my approach to leadership made the university better. Since I believe one's approach to leadership is informed by their lived experiences, is it plausible to reason that there are leadership characteristics generalizable to leaders who are LGBTQ or what could be called LGBTQ leadership "characteristics"? While this notion is often presented by LGBTQ leaders, scholars, and others, it is usually intended to summarize the leadership approaches of the growing numbers of leaders who are publicly identifying as LGBTQ and who are now being recognized as a distinct group. The question to consider is, to what extent, if any, are there leadership characteristics specifically attributable to LGBTQ leaders?

If we were to acknowledge that there are LGBTQ leadership characteristics, how would we come to know them as distinguishable from the general run-of-the-mill leadership qualities? The truth is that there are tremendous differences within the LGBTQ communities, and thus one would expect tremendous differences in our approaches to leadership. What if actually there are no inherent LGBTQ leadership characteristics? This is particularly plausible when one considers the intersectionality that exists with each of us nesting our identities within identities.

Appreciating intersectional identities becomes even more difficult in trying to offer a generalizable laundry list of leadership characteristics attributable to a "LGBTQ identity." For example, the way in which a tall, thin, white, gay man in his forties leads will be different from a short, not-so-thin white, lesbian woman in her sixties (this would be me). We would have different lived experiences and thus different approaches to leadership. The differences arise because our life's journey will have been fundamentally different, and the way people act and react to us will be different. We do, however, share leading as LTBTQ educators in a predominantly non-LGBTQ world.

What if there are no inherent LGBTQ leader characteristics but there is a LGBTQ leadership "style" based upon the LGBTQ leader's reaction to or navigation of the dominant patriarchal and heterosexist society that contextualizes how we lead? Navigation is how we act and react to our others. Think of it as if you are sailing a ship from one port to another and you have to navigate the rough seas and many hazards to get to your destination. The real LGBTQ leadership "style" is not a laundry list of usually desirable leadership characteristics that any leadership scholar would deem markers for quality. In actuality, the core of a LGBTQ leadership style is what every LGBTQ leader does to navigate a patriarchal, gendered, heterosexist culture. Those skills of successful navigation are the actual elements of what connects LGBTQ leaders and are thus the foundation of "our" style. Awareness, understanding, and perfecting how we successfully navigate the dominant culture's structures of power and privilege forms the basis of an LGBTQ leader-navigator style. LGBTQ leader-navigators use their constructed approach to leadership to navigate through the dominant culture. This might be the common thread that connects us to our very diverse LGBTQ culture.

Successful LGBTQ leaders possess an awareness of their existence within and outside of the dominant culture. Through this cultural understanding, coupled with both life and leader experiences, the leader-navigator creates and perfects their style within a context that manages the patriarchal, gendered, and heterosexist structures of power, privilege, and bias. As such, the LGBTQ leader does not possess universal LGBTQ-specific characteristics. They possess leadership characteristics that exist within a leader-navigator framework. The LGBTQ leader-navigator knows they are living and leading in a time that has been filled with a history and culture of contempt for LGBTQ folk. They know they exist outside of the majority culture. They know that they came to owning their LGBTQ identity with risk and courage. They also know that they own many other identities as well.

As an out "lesbian president," I accessed my leader-navigator style daily. This approach to leadership was also informed by my learning that the more one's identity is different from that of the dominant group, the easier it is for that difference to be the basis for hate by mean, bigoted, or unhinged individuals as they choose their form of attack. College presidents inevitably come under attack as they do their jobs. It is not about *if* but rather *when* and *how* these attacks will occur and how leaders navigate through them. As an LGBTQ president with a wonderful spouse who was highly engaged as a presidential spouse, we served a remote rural public regional university and were very public figures in the community. By and large the appointment and the community were fabulous; but at the same time we experienced bigotry and hate. A common form of hate was expressed through anonymous snail mail. At first, the hate was because we were an unmarried same-sex couple living in the official university president's residence. Several years into our presidency, when our state legalized gay marriage, we married and then (not-surprisingly) received anonymous hate mail because we had married.

What was surprising was when the editor of the local town paper called me to inform me that "an anonymous source" had found out about the marriage and that he was calling to investigate the anonymous source's allegation of an alleged impropriety. I thought this was the oddest phone call of my life. Instead of rage, I simply said that Peggy and I would be in his office in an hour and that we were more than ready to be interviewed. The reporter's contempt for us was made clear when his concluding question was: Why did you get married? After we got over the surprise of such an obtuse question, our answer was: Because we love each other. The editor printed this question and our answer in the article. In the end, the local paper ran a rather average article about gay marriage, the national movement, and statewide efforts as the backdrop to reporting on our marriage. After the interview, we braced for more hate; instead, we began receiving unsolicited wedding gifts, cards, and congratulations from civic and business leaders and regular folk, including well-wishes from the local senior citizen center. The article actually ignited conversations across the campus and community. This was an example of navigating hate into an opportunity for engagement and learning. Today this university is considered to be a very LGBTQ-friendly university by several outlets that rate such experiences.

This search for the common thread could well inform future leaders and leadership development programs. Simply asking LGBTQ leaders to talk about their approach to leadership without framing their leadership within "navigating the dominant cultural lens" is a missed opportunity for a truly informed discussion. Most leadership development programs leave out the cultural context, but it is one of the first topics that should be addressed. Understanding what forms successful leadership matters, and understanding what is common to LGBTQ leadership success matters. Looking at the LGBTQ leadership style as a style based on reacting to or navigating the power structures that dominate our culture is essential to fully describing the LGBTQ leader's approach to leading. Understanding the likelihood that during your presidency there will inevitably be moments when you will need to be prepared to "lead through the hate." While preparing for a presidency, it is important to consider how to plan for these often defining moments. This sharper awareness also provides an opportunity to inform leader preparation programs in ways that could increase LGBTQ leader success. Engaging and supporting LGBTQ leaders is important in that we are part of the diversity of thought and action needed for colleges and universities to achieve their priorities and overcome challenges.

Raymond E. Crossman

Growing up queer, I never believed I would be a leader. Growing up as a gay man in the 1980s in New York City, I never believed I would live past 30.

I now believe I am a leader because I am queer. Certainly, how I lead is determined by being gay. I'm alive and continue to learn.

I see myself as a reference rather than as an authority on LG-BTQ leadership. I am a gay, white, financially secure, cisgender male, living with HIV since the 1980s, born in 1964 on the cusp between the baby boomer and Generation X cohorts. These and other identities give me a particular expression of queer leadership that may not be relevant to those who come out before, after, or differently than me.

Queer scholars have helped me find my voice as a gay leader, but I don't work from any specific model of queer leadership. I do believe my leadership is stronger when I pay attention to its queer sources and conventions.

I am a product of the contrast that occurred between my childhood and professional eras.

As a child, in the 1970s, I was bullied physically and psychologically in school. Due in part to a brutishly obvious rhyme, I was widely known as "Gay Ray," at a time when "gay" was the ultimate derogative for a male. I yearned to be more fully known and understood, but I kept myself separate from others out of fear of greater levels of torment, which in retrospect seems ridiculous because everyone seemed to know I was gay. Yet I kept myself back from some of the basic social and developmental experiences one needs to grow up; academically, my performance was sufficiently compromised that I had to fight my way out of special education and remedial classroom placements.

Professionally, coming of age in the 1990s, I was a member of the first generation of queer people who were able to be somewhat comfortably out in graduate school, first jobs, and leadership roles in higher education. Certainly, I was heckled in graduate school by some peers and faculty, and I faced heterosexism in my first professional roles. But unlike the generation immediately prior—my senior peers who had bricks thrown through their office and residential windows—the bricks thrown at me in professional settings were metaphorical. I don't mean to minimize the hurt and pain of the 1990s: AIDS and death surrounded me, and I expected to be dead within a few years. But I worked hard during my early professional years to compartmentalize my pain, and I found some refuge in those years of beginning societal change.

This cusp—between persecution in childhood and some tolerance (yet not acceptance) as a young adult—led to specific ways of leading. I believe too this sequence gives me some ability to flex my queerness and to consider its implications for my leadership. I'll speak here to three leadership behaviors: my queer intuition, my reach for the fabulous, and my willingness to be a mess.

My early years of abuse led to an awareness of what oppression and privilege look like and mean. I developed a heightened sensitivity and prescience for what may be imminent, hidden, or overlooked. As a child, and then as a young person, this meant incessantly scanning my environment—both to avoid danger and to find queer people and camouflaged markers of queer culture. Now, as a leader, it's an automatic reaching to find the outlier idea or voice, the hidden resource, the fabulous. If something is associated with the majority culture or considered to be conventional wisdom, my first impulse is to run away, subvert, or re-appropriate. If there's a minority report or dissenting opinion, I want to read it. This is how I understand the development of what I'll call my superpower of queer intuition.

Social changes during my early professional years allowed me to dare to explore this queer intuition in service of being professionally creative. In the 1990s, I bounced out of my childhood with anger about my oppression, a curiosity about my talents, and a calling to do something about the machine that was killing so many of the gay men of my generation. Structural heterosexism dominated every context, and I had enough internalized heterosexism to temper my clarity about my calling and to make me reluctant to fully lead in my first leadership job in the late 1990s. But these years were also the beginning of my vision of the fabulous—a need to be political, transgressive, and courageous in my life and leadership.

My fabulousness comes from my struggle of living in a heteronormative world, but my fabulousness is not only driven by oppression. It also comes from finding and loving myself on the dance floor and in the professional world. Tony Kushner writes, "The fabulous is . . . the rapturous embrace of difference, the discovering of self not in that which has rejected you but in that which makes you unlike, and disliked, the Other" (Kushner 1996, vii). Being gay propelled me to work to be fabulous, which eventually drove me to have the audacity to accept a presidency at age 38.

This process—a course of self-discovery and working it out in a heteronormative world without LGBTQ precedents—was inherently and consistently messy. Higher ed presidencies are not designed to reward authenticity and vulnerability, but I've slowly realized the power of vulnerable leadership as an antidote to my closed and solitary childhood. I noticed early in my presidency that things went better when I talked about my process openly. Acting reliably on this realization is a challenge. But after I made the professional disclosure of my HIV status three years ago, I've been surprised that my queer intuition is clearer and that I can better reach for the fabulous. When I step forward also with the queer exuberance that is distinctive to the culture of gay men my age, I am better able to appreciate and support others with whom I serve.

I am a leader because I am gay, my leadership is distinctively queer, and I am better when I consciously make use of my queerness as a resource. Many LGBTQ leaders, including the fabulous contributors to this volume, vary in the degree to which they believe there is even such a thing as LGBTQ leadership. I believe we have much to learn from other identity groups, such as women and people of color, who seem more willing to say there's such a thing as female, Black, or Latinx leadership. And at the same time, the meaning and intersectionality of all social identities is changing. My LGBTQ generation seems to fight assimilation more than the generation coming of age now. Perhaps what I'm calling queer leadership will become a footnote, because the social determinants of it are certainly in transition. I'll be proud if the legacy of current LGBTQ leaders for future generations is that fabulousness becomes ubiquitous. For now, our work is not done, and LGBTQ leadership is well suited to a higher education system in search of new and more inclusive solutions.

REFERENCE

Kushner, T. 1996. Notes toward a Theater of the Fabulous. In *Staging Gay Lives: An Anthology of Contemporary Gay Theater*, ed. John M. Clum. Boulder, CO: Westview.

CHAPTER 2

Feminist Leadership

With respect, we acknowledge that there has been much thinking and writing about the relationship between leadership and gender, ethnicity, and marginalized identity status for both leaders and followers. We are all feminists, and if there is such a thing as "LGBTQ leadership," it became recognizable only after feminism became a force. The first writer in this chapter, Katherine Hancock Ragsdale, who led a divinity school, and the third writer, Erika Endrijonas, who leads a community college, parse the intersection of their lesbian and feminist identities. Both assert that sexism trumps heterosexism, and each explores responsibilities and outcomes that follow from intersectionality. The second contributor is Terry L. Allison, a gay man who led a public university, and he describes his discovery of feminism and how it has defined his leadership.

Katherine Hancock Ragsdale

Is it homophobia or misogyny? I think, feel, and believe that I encounter more roadblocks, more oppressive discrimination, more daily insults and indignities as a woman than I do as a queer person. But I can't know that for sure, as I've never lived any alternatives. Which is harder: life as a gay man or as a straight woman? This lesbian has an opinion but just can't know. Nor can I experience or fully know how white privilege has mitigated the difficulties that being gay and female have imposed. Nor will I ever decipher all the nuances of being a first-generation college graduate and a professional from a working-class background, having lived no other life with which to compare this one.

As a devotee of standpoint theory, I willingly acknowledge that I can only fully know what is visible and experienced from the point at which I stand and through the lenses I wear—and that my own understanding is made fuller and more complex by hearing others describe the view from their own perches. That is to say, my conclusions are limited by the perspectives to which I have access. Be that as it may, I do conclude that misogyny has a more pervasive negative impact on my life than does homophobia. In fact, from where I stand, it appears that homophobia is really a subset of misogyny.

Rooted in a misogynist patriarchy, homophobic men hate and fear gay men for subverting the paradigm of male dominance by entering into sexual and domestic relationships that either cast a man in a subservient, "womanly," position or (gasp) don't require a subservient partner at all. Lesbians, when we are noticed at all, tend to be deplored predominantly for not needing men to survive or even flourish. In both cases, the foundation of patriarchy—male dominance and female submission—is undermined. Even so, male privilege remains. I offer three, among hundreds, stories to illustrate.

A few decades ago, in the 1990s, a professor at a divinity school in Chelsea (NYC) found himself awake in the wee hours of the morning and decided that he may as well walk to the local hospital and visit a student with AIDS who he knew didn't sleep well. On his way there, a car full of teenage boys pulled alongside him and asked for directions to the Village, which he gave. Only as the car pulled away did he notice the New Jersey tags and realize that those boys were probably headed to the Village to "beat up some gays"—a fad among some New Jersey high-school boys at the time—and that he was lucky they hadn't assaulted him, a gay man.

The next day, at lunch in the dining hall, this professor railed at the state of a world in which he couldn't walk down the street without fear of being attacked. The women at the table looked on at a loss for words. Yes, of course, beating up, or just threatening, gay men is terrible, but what male privilege this professor took for granted. He was utterly oblivious to the fact that no woman in the room, gay or straight, would *ever*—even for a moment—imagine that it was safe to walk down the streets of New York City, alone, at 1 a.m.—would *ever* assume that a car pulling alongside her held men with benign intentions.

Also in the 1990s, a group of lesbian and gay Episcopal priests was discussing the ethics of the closet—knowing that being out was good for the movement but that it could well compromise individuals' ability to find jobs. One of the men raged that he had been out during his ordination process; that the ordination had been a locus of a great deal of publicity and controversy within the church; and that, therefore, he had probably forfeited his chance of becoming a bishop someday. He insisted that everyone, including a couple of closeted lesbians, should have to come out—in order to level the playing field. The lesbians, again, were stunned into silence. This guy, a perfectly nice guy but one of only average talent, assumed that, were it not for homophobia and heterosexism, he would of course advance to a prestigious position. At the time even super-star women, straight or gay, stood little to no chance of rising to the high offices for which they were more than qualified. Being out lesbians would make achieving even the entry-level positions *that this man already had* hard to come by. He was, I believe, correct in assuming that, as more and more people came out, the field on which gay and straight men played would become, if not level, then at least a bit closer to it. But the field on which he competed with both lesbian and straight women would become even more skewed in his favor, which, perhaps, felt more "normal" and, therefore, more fair to him.

Finally, when I was chosen to serve as president of Episcopal Divinity School (EDS), the board, rightfully, congratulated themselves for its willingness to call the first openly LGBTQ president of an Episcopal graduate school. I'm told that they concluded the meeting by encouraging one another to go face down the hostile homophobes who were sure to attack.

And there *were* attacks: picketing by the notorious anti-gay activist Fred Phelps, insulting headlines across the globe. Some of the headlines noted that EDS had called a lesbian to the presidency (or, as one put it, "EDS calls fat, angry, dyke"; I resisted the impulse to feed the trolls by replying that I wasn't angry). But what really had people upset was my history of abortion rights work. The board was completely unprepared (despite the fact that I was the first woman to head this school, and only the second woman ever to head any such school) for the sexist response.

They had, apparently, missed the memo about homophobia as a subset of misogyny. Or, perhaps, had never considered that it was this same misogynist patriarchy that fueled the opposition to reproductive choice for women. Women who control their own reproductive lives control their own destinies in ways that undermine dependence on, and subservience to, men. Hence the outrage—not at the school's hiring a lesbian (that generally only came up as a convenient "insult"), but rather at its hiring someone who had spent a lifetime undermining patriarchy by fighting for women's rights.

Clearly, our gay brothers are also victims of a misogyny that villainizes them for not appropriately supporting the patriarchy and defines them, therefore, as gender traitors. At the same time, gay men also carry male privilege. This privilege, to which too many of our gay brothers have been blind, can make working with them a fraught enterprise for lesbians. As, I would imagine, white privilege makes working with white LGBTQ or feminist colleagues fraught for our colleagues of color. It's hard not to be jealous of and angry about the privilege that they take for granted as they claim equivalent victimhood. Throw class into the mix, after determining how even to define class (current salary, level of education, parents' education, the neighborhood one grew up in, grandparents' wages or education . . . ?) and the complexities of privilege, as well as the potential resentments when the privilege/victim cards are played, grow exponentially. The potential for one's own experience of oppression to blind him to his advantages and the expense they impose on colleagues as well as competitors is huge and multifaceted.

On the other hand, those who really get it—who note both their own privilege and the shared frustrations and outrage at being overlooked, undervalued, and victimized—those brothers can be strong allies and reliable friends. Acknowledging and inhabiting the complexities of these relationships serve as a constant reminder of the importance of making space for other voices to be fully heard and for not assuming a parity, or similarity of experience, that others may not feel or believe. Working through these complexities can build sustaining and world-changing alliances and make each of us better at our shared work of making justice. It also stands to make us better leaders. We, whose lives have been so pervasively shaped by multiple, intersecting identities and oppressions, should know a great deal about the importance of fully hearing a multitude of voices—and of allowing those diverse voices to shape out worldview. The importance of a leadership style that makes space— welcoming, appreciative space—for such voices is not foreign to us.

The high-profile nature of a presidency provides a rare opportunity to explore and model strong commitments to such authentic and aware collegiality in a very public way. These commitments have been foundational principles of feminism for decades. LGBTQ alliances, at their best, are built upon similar awareness and commitment. Having navigated the varied assortment of privileges and challenges we each, individually, face to achieve a presidency and, therefore, the opportunity to influence the culture that shapes us and those who will follow, is one of the compelling gifts the vocation offers.

Terry L. Allison

In a 2004 issue of the *Journal of Homosexuality*, Robert Jensen wrote: "I have not met many gay men who are willing to publicly identify with (or sometimes even engage in) the radical feminist critique, and use that framework to analyze gay culture" (Jensen 2004). More recently, in a Pride Month *Los Angeles Times* op-ed titled "Gay Men Need to Be Feminists, Too," Rich Benjamin found similar circumstances:

> Gay men shouldn't dominate the debate, but neither should we hang back in apathy, fatigue or fear of saying the wrong thing. The post-gay, post-work, post-feminist movements might sound fashionable, but the spate of anti-women legislation demands we show up for women. Gay men may have become more liberated, but feminism hasn't run its course. (Benjamin 2019)

In contrast, my own experience of gay male leadership in higher education, as well as that of some of my peers, has been built upon feminist principles and practices learned both from lived experience and from academic study.

My awakening to linked homophobia and misogyny was sustained, painful, and cruelly illuminating. Living in a small town in central California between the ages of 12 and 17, I was relentlessly bullied for perceived gender nonconformity. My fellow students put me through constant verbal and intermittent physical abuse. At times I literally walked a gauntlet, frightened that someone would push me or "call me out" for a fight. I was told that I walked, talked, giggled, acted, thought, behaved, threw, ran "like a girl."

My initial reactions went something like this: "I'm not trying to do anything 'like' anyone else. This is who I am. Why do people hate me so?" Without the benefit of formal study, I understood that many young men in particular wanted everyone to act within defined gender roles, but I didn't get why they were so invested in this enterprise. I had only the vaguest notion that gays or lesbians existed and certainly did not understand that there were gay or lesbian couples or communities. (This was the period from 1968 to 1973.) By my junior year in high school I began to grasp that the hatred was directed not only at the idea that I was "*like* a girl," exhibiting inappropriate gender behavior, but also directed at "like a *girl*." I came to understand the level of contempt directed at the feminine. It was an emotionally and psychically expensive form of consciousness raising, but the lesson was profound. The insight that misogyny was at the core of this hatred led me to feminism. I started attending girl's athletic events as spectator, deliberately working with female classmates on projects, and following the women's movement.

Although my deliverance from a rural high school to the University of California, Berkeley provided great freedom, it provided few opportunities to study gender and no opportunities that I knew of to study sexuality. (I was at Berkeley from 1973 to 1983. I audited what may have been the first sociology class offered on "homosexuality" in the early 1980s.) It was only a decade after finishing my undergraduate degree, when I began my master's then doctoral work in literature at University of California, San Diego, that I began to develop my academic understanding of feminism as a basis for sexuality or queer studies. In the meantime, as a faculty member at a new campus (California State University, San Marcos), I was invited to teach in the women's studies program, bringing recent research into gay and lesbian studies. It was within this context that I was able for the first time to link my leadership practices with feminist principles. While serving as vice president of our faculty union, I was approached by two recent hires in a department, both young women, about their perception of gender discrimination in pay. As an academically trained feminist, I used my research skills to investigate. While we could not demonstrate a campus-wide pattern of discrimination, we were able to prove that these two women had a case, and they were granted back pay and a permanent increase. My interest in feminist research as a gay man who had linked homophobia and misogyny eventually had a direct, applied result that benefited women. I began to see how feminist principles could guide my university leadership practices, and eventually became co-chair, then the chair, of the Women's Studies Program at California State San Marcos.

My academic training in feminism also helped me to distinguish between oppressive systems of patriarchy, race, and class (among others), and individual leadership skills or behaviors. The relative independence in thinking and action of the professoriate can sometimes mask the patriarchal structures that influence the institution. The assertion of independence and the collective authority embodied in the academic senate does not mean that the academy has freed itself of patriarchal or other power structures. In one management position, I found myself simultaneously dealing with four cases in three different departments of female graduate students sexually involved with male professors. In each case, the fallout for the graduate student from the breakup of these relationships was significant to her course of study. I brought my gay male feminism to the table when I addressed this cluster of activity not just as individual decisions or failures, but as a structural problem.

Being a gay male feminist leader also has helped me not to sentimentalize or demonize any one leader based on group affiliation. For me, the best bosses, female or male, have applied feminist principles: inclusion; truly giving voice to individuals; recognizing diversity of approach and differing needs; allowing independence and authority while requiring accountability; accepting a reasonable amount of error if it leads to deeper learning. Some of my female colleagues and I have remained committed to feminist leadership even when we have experienced a female leader who betrayed each of these principles.

My own biggest challenge in feminist leadership came early in my time as chancellor of Indiana University South Bend and lingered throughout my service. Toward spring break, the president of the Student Government Association (SGA) told me that with declining enrollment, the SGA had chosen to withdraw their already reduced support of the childcare service on campus. As a gay feminist leader, I was committed to providing support to assist women attending school. I also was committed to giving students real choices with their budgets and not overriding their decisions. What happens when two feminist principles conflict?

In a series of meetings over several years, I did the best I could to use the feminist principles I brought to the table. I asked to meet with a philosophy professor who taught feminist philosophy for advice about what questions I might ask of myself and others during the decision-making process. I tried to understand the structure of the SGA to see whether working adult women students were included. I gathered information about who used the childcare center and whether we had evidence of its success in keeping students in school. I also looked at competing needs that had been expressed as priorities of students, faculty, and staff. Soon, the childcare center was outsourced, and we were able to sustain it for three somewhat difficult years. Centrally, for me, the center no longer had an academic function, so in looking at additional required investment, I couldn't justify its further operation. Although I had tried to employ feminist principles and practices, many faculty and students on our campus perceived the actions as unsupportive of women students and the opposite of feminist leadership.

Whether or not I succeeded in this particular case, my academic training in feminism shaped my leadership practices as a gay male leader in academia. From my own observations, my gay male colleague deans, provosts, presidents, and chancellors have been much more aware of and committed to feminist principles and practices than is suggested by the statements that began this brief essay. As the number of gay male leaders in academia grows, more research on our knowledge, attitudes, and skills in feminism would be most welcome.

REFERENCES

Benjamin, R. June 23, 2019. Gay Men Need to Be Feminists, Too. *Los Angeles Times*.

Jensen, R. 2004. Homecoming: The Relevance of Radical Feminism for Gay Men. *Journal of Homosexuality* 47 (3/4): 79.

Erika Endrijonas

I've been a feminist longer than I have known what the word means. The nearest I can pinpoint my rejection of a world based on assumptions that men are leaders and women are helpers is when I was in seventh grade and I wasn't doing that well in school. For some reason, the transition from elementary school to junior high was harder than expected, and I just wasn't doing my work. My mother was none too thrilled and threatened that if I didn't get it together, the only college that would take me was the Bryman School, a proprietary medical secretarial school that promised to teach women to "learn to work in a doctor's world." That sent chills up my spine because I didn't see myself taking orders from doctors, who were all assumed to be men, of course. After all, it was the 1970s.

I'm no less resistant to a workplace permeated by gendered assumptions today, but the difference is that as president, it's my job to create an environment free of gendered expectations and sexism, not to mention racism, homophobia, and classism. I don't know if this is a fair expectation, but I feel it as a real responsibility and have for most of my professional life.

People often assume that being an out lesbian leader must be really hard. It's no cakewalk at times, but the truth is that I've experienced far more sexism in my career than I have homophobia. Even after being a college president at two different institutions, I have many things "man-splained" to me, and that doesn't even count the number of times that what I say is ignored until a male colleague says the exact same thing. I have also seen male colleagues forgiven for outbursts, including profanity, because they are "artists" and more prone to emotion. I told the person who offered that excuse to me that I doubted I would be afforded the same consideration if the situation were reversed.

I am definitely a dyke, but I don't really look like that stereo-type. Early into my first job at a community college, a male faculty member at the college just couldn't quite accept my sexual orien-tation, not because he was homophobic, but because he couldn't shake the idea that I just hadn't been with the right man yet. Males whom he thought were confidantes often shared his musings about "what if" he could "turn me." He wasn't the only one; a faculty member who reported to me offered his services more than once if I wanted to remind myself of what the other side was like. Even as an out lesbian and in a leadership position, I was still viewed as a conquest, but I chalked that up more to a standard objectification of me as a woman than to anything else.

Being a female leader requires a thick skin but also the willing-ness to call out sexism when and where it happens. I've lost count of the number of times I've had to correct people—both men and women—at all levels, including males I reported to, that tables are "staffed" not "manned" unless only men will be there. Similarly, I have had to, on more than one occasion, in public venues, call out egregious sexism. One of the most notable was a male board member, who listened to a male colleague and me as we each spoke to a staffing issue, and then characterized my arguments as "emo-tional" and my male colleague's as "logical." Without missing a beat, I chastised the board member for his sexist terms; thankfully, I was not the only person who recognized his comments as inap-propriate. Oh, and that was in 2018. We really haven't come very far.

Being a feminist leader also requires me to politely correct people in groups large and small, not to make anyone feel badly, but to show that sexist anything—language, behavior, humor—is simply not ok. When a male staff member accused me of "going politically correct" when I had to shut down comments in a meet-ing that could be interpreted as sexist and racist, I responded that ensuring that people are treated with dignity was simply correct, forget about the political. To this day, I don't think he understood what I meant.

I'm not just a feminist leader; I'm a lesbian feminist leader who understands what it feels like to be the "other," which I believe makes me sensitive to assumptions about who our students are and what they need to be successful. All of these anecdotes are merely examples of my personal experience, but they all fit into a larger picture. Feminist leadership is more than just "leaning in" and talking about the need to address inequality in all forms. In order to be an authentic feminist leader, I have to own my white privilege and take seriously my moral obligation to do better and to be better than the female and male leaders who came before me.

I have spoken at various conferences about leadership, and I am often asked how I became "me," an out leader who is unafraid to speak my mind. My response is that I believe leadership is about having the courage of conviction, and especially as a female leader, knowing my worth. When I interview for positions, I am clear that "what you see is what you get." I am outspoken and unafraid to say what's on my mind. I don't know how to be an out lesbian leader any other way, and the end result is that people always seem to rely on me to be the one who says what needs to be said.

In my first job at a community college, about two years into my tenure there, I was asked to serve on a diversity panel at a college professional development day about being out. As I made my way down to the stage to make my presentation, one of my male dean colleagues said, "I think I am about to watch you destroy your career." After what appeared be a successful turn on the panel, where I talked about the need to create an inclusive environment in the classroom and workplace by providing examples of some of the thoughtless things people had said to me at the college, that same dean told me that he had just witnessed my career take off. I think his original assumption was that sharing my experience would reveal my vulnerability, and, for him, vulnerability was a sign of weakness. Instead, what he realized was that being so honest was what made my presentation and, by extension, my work as a dean meaningful and effective.

Vulnerability is an expression of authenticity, both of which are components of how I define myself as a lesbian feminist leader. Who better to serve the most vulnerable than a leader who can identify with the experiences of our students and create an institution that works to empower them to succeed?

CHAPTER 3

Intersectionality and Leadership

How does our experience of seen and unseen identities contribute to our leadership, and how do others perceive us? Some of us have the experience of being summed up in terms of one of our identities, and some of us find ourselves complicit in the efficiency of higher education, which does not grapple with intersectionality. In this chapter, we extend our consideration to some of the many parameters that contribute to leadership, such as class, ethnicity, ability, health status, and age. All three contributors explore intersectionality—interconnected social categories such as race, gender, class, or ability that create overlapping and interdependent disadvantages—as an asset for leadership. DeRionne Pollard, president of a large community college, describes how she came to understand her intersectionality as a résumé to lead. Raymond E. Crossman, president of an urban private university, considers an ability and health status that has been largely unexplored in terms of leadership. Rusty Barceló, retired from the presidency of a public university, closes the chapter; she argues that intersectionality must be the core of the academy.

DeRionne Pollard

I grew up on the south side of Chicago, a racial and economically diverse jungle serrated along an infamous planning-grid design. As a child of Chicago, you identified and labeled yourself by the intersections that defined your existence. "Where do you live, DeRionne?" My response to you would likely be 79th and Wood. Where was my elementary school? 77th and Wolcott. My church? 84th and Ashland. Identity and wayfinding were always the combination of these intersections.

My best friend and later wife found this phenomenon of "intersectional self-identification" fascinating, so much so that she would pretend that she was from Chicago by making up intersections. She understood the archetype—but she didn't have the lived experience to give her intersections authenticity.

Intersections matter.

How one shows up in intersections matters as well. Familiar faces, maybe even friends, could be found at minor intersections, but major intersections brought you in contact with strangers as our directions collided in what could become unintended and unexamined possibilities and conflicts. As a black girl and then woman, I quickly learned that intersections brought out the best and the worst in people. Intersections are unavoidable, yet one didn't typically dally in them.

To this day, in my world intersections are often messy, congested, and dangerous. They are verbs not nouns—they express a relationship between things as predicates do; intersections compound pressure, create tension, expand boundaries, and make complicated realities more complex. Crossing lived experiences and reconciling sameness, difference, and distinctiveness can be both magnifying and cataclysmic. The mere existence of intersections is not the issue—lines, things, streets, people, identities cross all the time—but the power of intersections is in their impact and influence.

Intersections matter.

So, the fall of 2010 found me starting my presidency of Montgomery College (MC), a community college in Maryland serving more than 50,000 students, I spent the greater part of my first semester simply learning about and absorbing the macro-culture of MC. Much like the streets of Chicago, I found the major and minor crossings, learned which thoroughfares provided literal and figurative wayfinding, and came to know how to give meaning to what I observed and lived.

This particular day found me walking the halls of the Student Services Building on one campus. A small voice called my name. "Aren't you Dr. Pollard?" Growing accustomed to the glorious students who often stopped me to introduce themselves, I took in a beautiful, college-age Latino male, who reached out his hand to me with an incredulous look on his face.

He began by welcoming me to the community, and we chatted about the area and my explorations to that point. All of a sudden, he paused and focused his gaze on my feet. "I came out to my family," he spilled out. Tears began to roll down his cheeks, and I stepped closer into his space and grabbed his hands. It wasn't an unfamiliar experience, and I knew my job in that moment was simply to listen.

"Oh yeah? How'd that go?"

Looking directly at me, he responded, "Not so good." I'll never forget the story in his eyes as my own welled up in response to his undeniable pain and loneliness. Both of us stood in this hallway intersection, holding hands, and tears rolled down.

"My father won't talk to me, and my mother . . . well, she just can't understand why I felt the need to say anything. She said I've ruined my future, that I won't be able to have a career. I have so many things going against me, so why couldn't I just keep this to myself? That my life is over. That I won't be able to do or be anything."

I opened my mouth to try to offer some comfort, some insight about how this moment is significant but not defining . . . how there are so many role models whose lives are gloriously consequential and successful because of, in spite of, or even not impacted at all by their sexual identity. I scrambled to assemble words to capture my awareness of how race, gender, religion, sexuality, and economics were intertwined within his retelling, and I wanted to lift up his bravery, his strength, his resilience, and his gifts. I wanted to remind him that he mattered and that how he showed up from this point forward was important for him and those who were observing him. I wanted to tell him that he wasn't alone and that many of us stood in the junction with him.

Before I could form a cogent response, his face lit up with a radiant smile and his hold tightened on my hands. "But the day you were named president of Montgomery College, I ran home and showed my mother the announcement. I told her that I might not be able to be everything, but I can be a college president one day."

I don't know what folks made of us, the college president and the student standing in the intersection of two hallways crying and laughing, but for me this continues to be one of the most significant moments in my life. Leaning into those identities has made me more aware, more accessible, more effective as a college president as it has become my "why" in how I want to do this work. Embracing my intersectionality has liberated me and makes me a better human, leader, mentor, and student, so much so that I recently began introducing myself when speaking in this way: "First-generation college completer; proud Chicago public schools graduate; former food stamps and public assistance recipient; motherless child and boy mom healed by parenting; loved by and loving the most glorious woman in the world for nearly 30 years; and proud advocate for all things community college and the students and communities we serve."

Intersections matter.

My time with that student left me changed. How many of our students needed to see LGBTQI folks in our community? How many couldn't conceive of their future because those of us who'd stood in the intersections hadn't shared our stories in ways that could have impact and influence? What would it take to make that happen? Building on the college's proud tradition of a series of photography exhibitions called *Portraits of Life,* in which we explored the lived experiences of Holocaust survivors and global student experiences, we raised private dollars and commissioned a new series called *Portraits of Life: LGBT Stories of Being.* The exhibition was a collection of words and photographs "portraying lesbian, gay, bisexual, and transgender community members who contribute to the quality of life in Montgomery County, Maryland through their everyday activities." Included were elected politicians, religious leaders, business owners, veterans, attorneys, activists, laborers, arts leaders, and more—and this college president.

At the opening of the exhibition two years later, I offered comments, as college presidents are wont to do at this type of event: I told how we raised the support for it, and I shared an abbreviated version of my hallway interaction with the student. Seeing and being seen for those students and community members who need to see LGBTQI members of their community leading, serving, working, and living—that was the purpose of this exhibition. As I left the podium, I felt a hand gently clasping mine, and imagine my surprise: there was my inspirational student, whom I had not seen since our conversation in the hallway.

The tears were different this time.

Raymond E. Crossman

I may be writing in the wrong book. Because I wonder whether my identity as a person living with HIV since the 1980s informs my leadership more than does my identity as queer.

I may also be writing in the wrong chapter. Because as a white cisgender man, I should be *asking* questions about intersectionality rather than speaking to them.

The reason I am writing here is that I believe that I've consistently underestimated how HIV—as an ability and health status and as a life experience—has shaped me as a leader. I believe, too, that this has generally been rarely described or acknowledged. For me, the effects of my identities as gay and as living with HIV both intersect and remain distinct.

I've been out as queer professionally since graduate school, but I've only been out as a person living with HIV professionally for the past three years, since 2017. Family and many friends knew about my HIV status, but until recently I kept my story under wraps at work. I don't know whether the board that hired me would have hired me into a presidency in 2003 had they known about my HIV status. But I decided for them with my silence.

Across those early years of my presidency, when I was loud about the gay but closeted about the HIV, I led a good deal of social justice work at my institution. I felt enormously grateful for the opportunity to bring to my work what I learned as a young man living with HIV in the 1980s in New York City and in the 1990s in Atlanta. In the 1980s and even in the 1990s, I heard almost every day that I deserved to die because I was gay. I gained much experience with oppression and injustice, and I developed skill in conceptualization and advocacy. Now in the 2000s, I was able to apply what I had learned with students, faculty, administration, and trustees within a higher education context. Sweet.

Sometimes, I'd experience pushback about my intentions. I'd hear incredulity that the administration would want to tackle issues of justice. I wondered how I'd become The Man. I'd think, but never share, "Don't you know my credentials to do this work?" In retrospect, I believe that my reaction was determined partly by white privilege and white fragility. But also, the truth was: no, my community did not know my credentials to do this work because I was hiding an essential part of my experience that fueled my interest and ability to pursue issues of social justice.

My decision to come out of hiding was not an attempt to clean up my act as a leader. Rather, I was driven by an uneasy feeling of déjà vu following the 2016 presidential election. In 1985, the sitting president's refusal to speak the word *AIDS* caused my community injury and death. In 2017, the new president's incendiary words caused injury and death. I wondered whether many immigrants—and many people who might look like immigrants—felt as I did in the 1980s. I couldn't know the contemporary experience of many marginalized groups. But I could imagine that many people—Muslims, women, people living with disabilities, people of color standing up against structural racism, people at the intersection of these and many more identities—felt as abandoned by the state as I felt then.

I decided that my status and my story are what I had to offer. My community saved itself from extinction in the face of government-sanctioned indifference, hatred, and oppression. I not only survived the plague but achieved some measure of success, as a university president, perhaps in part because of what I had learned in surviving. So I came out.

I came out as big as I could, as the first university president to do so. I wrote in the popular press; I did a junket. The response was enormously positive inside my university and around the world. I believe that coming out has had positive effect on my leadership as well. It is not the case that everyone now gets me. Alas. It is also not the case that I don't have a great deal of continuing work to do as a white man in the president's seat—to engage questions about my privilege on an ongoing basis. I *can* say that I'm now more comfortable in my role and that I know that I'm doing important work to support authentic dialogue, challenge my own and others' privilege, and advance justice.

Only now that I've leveled the field between the gay and the HIV can I begin to understand the relative and related contributions of these to my leadership. I think it might look the same to naive observers, but I realize it's not.

I'll try to explain through the most relevant metaphor to members of my tribe: dance.

I learned to dance at the height of the AIDS crisis in the late 1980s and early 1990s among and from a small community of men. When I dance today, when I get the rare chance, I dance exactly how I danced then. And, if you see me on the dance floor, you can definitely tell I'm gay. Please. But what you may not be able to notice is how much HIV determines my dance. I can tell you, even though I don't ever really think or talk about this, which of my steps are from which dance partner, the most important of whom are men who died of HIV. I could also tell you, in this indelicate unpacking of my groove, which steps are my own, uncopied from others, but rather are moves, gestures, and invocations that I developed in the 1980s and '90s to ward off oppression, fear, and death. There's a way that I swing my fist that means "I'm strong" or "stay away," depending on how I do the swing. There's a way that I point up to the sky that means hope. I spin, stomp, and pace in different ways to regulate whether I need to look inside for strength or outside to find or offer strength. In the 1980s and '90s, we danced to keep each other alive, as well as for those who were taken from us— and if you know what to look for, you can see all that in my dance.

Dancing is leading and leading is dancing. My metaphor isn't a metaphor at all. And if I unpack my contemporary dance as president, you can see the gay in my leadership. Please. But the HIV is as visible if you know how to look.

Some leadership elements are dually determined. When I work to incorporate voices across our university into decisions, and the extent to which I'm good at it, it's because I recall my own disconnection and bullying as a gay kid, but it's also because I'm keenly aware of how diminished we were and are when voices are taken away or disappeared. I continue to learn that today as loved ones continue to die from HIV.

Some of my leadership is queer and then jet-fueled by HIV. My creativity and fabulousness as a leader have developed in part because I was denied routine developmental experiences and was othered while growing up gay. My fabulousness as a leader then kaleidescoped after I learned from HIV how to fight for my life—not only surviving but thriving because of my experiences.

But then there's how my sense of responsibility elevates my reasoning to go beyond myself and my own experiences. My responsibility is to those who died and will continue to die. That's all HIV.

Rusty Barceló

I write as a queer Chicana who has lived on the margins—not only of the broader academy but also of spaces we share and do not share. Even as a president, I lived on from the margins as a Chicana queer woman—perceived as "other" by many, including people of color, the women community, and the queer community.

The issue of my identity has been an ongoing one as each community that I represent—queer, women, Chicano/a, and people of color—has tried to claim one part of me but seldom as a whole, Chicana queer disabled woman.

This failure to recognize and respect the intersectionality and fluidity of multiple identities has caused friction within communities as I have attempted to interact with each community. This keeps some of us on the margins of our affinity groups, making us feel unsafe in spaces where we should feel most comfortable. It has subjected some of us to violence and led to the ranking of oppressions, playing into the destructive us-versus-them tropes of the dominant culture. Despite these obstacles, we have found opportunities on our own and in collaboration with others to ensure our recognition and empowerment in the academy.

Over the years, I've built up a kind of mettle enabling me to find my voice and speak out as a queer Chicana, even when it was risky to do so. I've learned to be "reasonable," professional," and restrained even when I ache to strike out.

In a gendered, homophobic, and racialized world, it's a constant struggle as an academic female leader who is both Chicana and queer, to manage the indignities of daily living while keeping my composure. As I navigated the academy, I endured, and witnessed, microaggressions, even as I strove to be disciplined and evenhanded, inhabiting an in-between space of tensions and contradictions, a space where differences constantly intersect and collide.

I have learned through the years that positional leadership is important, but it's not enough. We need to lead differently based on identity in light of the current state of affairs nationally. We need to stop replicating existing systems of power and privilege. These systems may reward us with presidencies, but they are also the very systems that excluded us from being "out," increasing our marginalization.

Neither the numbers nor the climate for queer people of color has changed much over the past decade, especially for academic leaders. However, as our nation becomes more diverse, we will all have to be multiculturalists—meaning inclusive of *all* groups and recognizing the salience of intersectionality calling for new forms of leadership. As academic leaders, we must model multicultural leadership by breaking out of comfort zones, to embrace diversity and work across cultural differences. If we can't figure out how to do it, then how can we expect our institutions to change?

When I was young, I never thought that I would be an academic leader, much less a college president. But I attribute any success I have enjoyed as I moved up the ladder to maintaining my values, which are embedded in my identities. In fact, a principle that guides my work: True leadership comes from the heart. Whatever kind of leader we aspire to be, we must draw from our identities, our values, and our deepest well of strength.

Once after a keynote address focusing on women, an African American woman who said she had been following my career path asked how it was that I was able to keep my identity and values intact as a woman of color. Frankly, I had never thought of it before that moment; but I have done lots of thinking about it since.

I came to understand that if our leadership is inauthentic, we might make it to the top of the power hierarchy, and we might have formal authority over others. But we won't lead with integrity. We will be a boss, not a leader. We will leave parts of ourselves behind. And we will probably be unhappy.

We need to ask: If we don't change systems of oppression because we have acquiesced, what have we accomplished besides our own individual advancement—and at what cost? And if we don't change the system—who will? If you ask colleagues, they'll tell you: "I didn't get here by keeping my identities in a closet or limiting my voice. I was often a thorn in the side of colleagues, as were my friends and allies, many of whom came into the academy from the margins."

Without our critique of higher education, it would have kept us on the margins, shouting at the people in power. We learned how to negotiate. We learned what we needed to do to gain legitimacy in the academy and work within the system. We never lost sight of who we were, and we never lost our edge of critique. As leaders, that edge made us change agents, not accomplices.

The net result of our efforts is a new kind of academy, with women's studies, ethnic studies, and gender studies, equal opportunity policies, a transformed curriculum, and a changing student and faculty profile; a system in which a queer Chicana can become a college president, not by playing by the old rules, but by changing the rules; and not in spite of who she is, but because of who she is.

Consequently, we need to rethink, reimagine, and build on this work. This requires bringing all voices to the table and engaging everyone in decision-making across a multitude of differences. This new kind of leadership supports individual effort and achievement, but more importantly, it shares the responsibility and the rewards across complex, interlocking systems of culture and thought.

If I seem to have the courage of my convictions, it's perhaps because I was raised to be who I was—and I certainly was not the typical little girl. I'll tell you a story I often share: when I had polio at the age of 6, my parents presented me with a remarkable gift. The gift was an acknowledgment of who I am and not who they wanted me to be. I'll never forget the joy I felt, in spite of being paralyzed, when Dad presented me with a toy cowboy gun holster set, which

Mom buckled around my waist. That was the first of many acts of validation from my parents and other family members over the years—acts that reinforced my identity and confidence. Their affirmation has been with me throughout my academic career as an insider and outsider: People expect me to be strong and commanding but also deferential: acting with institutionally assigned authority while also "knowing my place" in the cultural and institutional hierarchy.

I realize I still make choices that leave me feeling fragmented and disoriented. There are few places where I can be Chicana and queer and feminist and professional and strong and vulnerable and forceful and loving . . . all at the same time, but I try. I know every time a person of color or a lesbian or a woman with a disability crosses a threshold, we all cross with her. When she is held back, we are all held back.

I hope to have played some part in transforming the academy to be more inclusive today although there is still much to do. However, I hope our work and our accomplishments of the last 50 years will be the foundation you need for a more inclusive and respectful academy with intersectionality of identities at its core.

CHAPTER 4

Coming Out and Being Out

Sharing coming out stories is a ritual that queer people often use to communicate all manner of information with each other and with others. The stories are instructive and often rich with nuance. This chapter offers those "campfire stories" and explores what coming out in a higher education presidency might mean, especially at this moment. How do we do it, when, and why? Some of us come out within many leadership interactions for different reasons—to model or to teach, to clarify consent or to avoid embarrassment, to challenge an assimilationist model, to provide a credential to increase our approachability or humanity. The first contributor, Ralph J. Hexter, formerly the president of a private liberal arts college and interim chancellor of a large public research university, and the second contributor, James Gandre, currently the president of an urban music conservatory, chronicle many personal and professional coming out stories and then offer examples of how they use coming out to lead. The third author, Regina Stanback Stroud, is the former chancellor of a community college district; she describes a journey of "never" or belatedly coming out personally and then selecting when to come out professionally in the context of institutional needs and her own intersectionality.

Ralph J. Hexter

If there is a single narrative that everyone, whatever their orientation, thinks of when they think about gay men and lesbians, it's the coming out story. Since 1988, National Coming Out Day has been held every October 11th, and its basic premise still holds true: When LGBT individuals remain hidden, they are invisible, and this allows the community at large to continue to assume that everyone is heterosexual and cisgender. Although there's a certain naive optimism in the assumption, the idea is that once the great majority realize that someone in their family or among their friends or work associates doesn't conform to standard expectations, they'll become tolerant.

Of course, it's not the case that "coming out" is an option for all LGBTQ individuals. Some likely face physical violence or economic catastrophe. All the more reason for those of us who have, for one reason or another, the privilege of coming out to do so. I am, and was, one of those individuals.

Though I had some anxiety about the decision at the time, in retrospect, it didn't cost me a great deal to come out when and where I did—in 1971 in Cambridge, Massachusetts, during my sophomore year at Harvard College. Yet it would be too simplistic to say that Cambridge was a liberal "bubble" and that the early 1970s were uniformly buoyed by the spirit of Stonewall. I recently had the opportunity to talk to a number of my college classmates. It is clear that there were many at the time who were terrified to come out—probably many more than the few of us who did.

While the threat of violence has not gone away, a significant difference between then and now is that it was much more possible then to come out in stages: first to close friends and then, more gradually and controllably, to a wider circle. Today, social media makes this impossible for all but the very few who refuse to have any digital presence at all. Hence the heartrending stories of young people who take their own lives when some aspect of their sexuality or gender identity is, against their will, shared online.

My experience and my views are inseparable from the realities of my place in the world and the times in which I have lived. Conceding, then, that my story is neither universal nor meant to be taken that way, let me explain how I navigated the ins and outs of coming out—from college years to the college presidency and beyond.

Already in my twenties, I had figured out that not everyone was as willing to be identified as gay as I was. For all sorts of reasons, probably deriving from my temperament and upbringing, I felt an obligation to be on the front lines. I also reasoned with myself that if I came out, I could be sure that any discrimination I experienced was "the real thing." Whereas if I stayed in the closet out of fear of possible negative impacts, I would end up inflicting on myself all the injuries that might never have materialized.

After graduating from Harvard, I spent three years in England, where the echoes of Stonewall were much fainter and, outside of London perhaps, the gay and lesbian presence was quite muted. Homosexual activity between consenting adults 21 or over had just been decriminalized in 1967, ten years after the publication of the astonishingly progressive Wolfenden Report. Nevertheless, while I was in England, Mary Whitehouse—Britain's answer to Anita Bryant—successfully sued the founding editor of *Gay News* for blasphemy. Meanwhile I remember "liberating" a few dances at my university, and I know the degree to which I and a few others were willing to be visible and out encouraged fellow students to express themselves and find their own voices.

Back in the United States and at Yale, following the lead of my friend, mentor, and eventually colleague John Boswell, author of *Christianity, Social Tolerance and Homosexuality* (1980) and *Same-Sex Unions* (1994), among other books, I was quite comfortable coming out and being out while still untenured. Even as an assistant professor, I expected that my partner would be included in social events on the same basis as my colleagues' other-sex partners; in one instance, this was an invitation to the home of the university president, and we prevailed.

At a certain point I came to question the need for me to come out again and again, in every new situation and with every new individual. "Why is the burden on me?," I asked myself. Not that it changed the way I functioned, but I shifted from thinking in terms of *coming* out to simply *being* out. In conversation I might simply drop a masculine pronoun in for my partner and put the work of accommodation on the person with whom I was talking. I still do this, even though now we can use the word *husband* to describe one another. If not coming out lets folks assume that being heterosexual and cisgender is "normal," my agenda is to remind people that they should not assume that everyone is paired with, or interested romantically in, a member of the "opposite sex"—a phrase itself now hopelessly outdated.

It might have been risky, but I made sure that no one ever hired me, for any position, without being fully aware of the fact that I was gay and openly so. I told myself that I wouldn't want to be at any institution that would regard this as a barrier, though of course I knew that I was extremely fortunate in being able to take so high-minded a stance. I hadn't planned on a career in higher administration, so it was only after several years as a dean of arts and humanities at the University of California, Berkeley, that the double-barreled thought occurred to me that, first, I was on a trajectory that might potentially lead to a presidency or chancellorship, and, second, that I knew no gay or lesbian people in those positions.

Between 2001 and 2005, I found myself confronting this classic "glass ceiling" problem. I organized a discussion of the issue at a meeting of Association of American University deans. At the same time, it happened that a number of liberal arts colleges on both coasts made overtures, and in 2005 Hampshire College in Amherst, Massachusetts, offered me the presidency. Hampshire College is well known for its progressive politics and commitment to social justice, so while I was by no means the first self-identifying gay president, Hampshire College may have been the first institution determined to make its incoming president's being gay an integral part of the public announcement. This was picked up by the press, perhaps most notably the *Los Angeles Times*, which ran a color photo of me and my partner on its front page.

More importantly, several of us out presidents found one another, and ultimately LGBTQ Presidents in Higher Education came into being.

Being out as a college or university president, or in any endeavor—among candidates for president of the United States to pick a random example—is important. It sends a message to people of every description that one can be open and honest about something that has been a matter of shame and in some eyes still is. Elsewhere in this volume, we discuss the particular qualities that being gay or lesbian bring to the college presidency. Here I would only say that being out is a guarantee of one's courage, one's honesty, and one's integrity. These are essential characteristics in a college or university leader, and when one stands up in public as a self-identifying LGBTQ individual, the world can be assured of the presence of those qualities.

Somewhere in Des Moines or San Antonio there is a young gay person who all of a sudden realizes that she or he is gay. Knows that if their parents find out they will be tossed out of the house. The classmates would torture the child. And the Anita Bryants and John Briggs are doing their bit on TV. That child has several options: staying in the closet or suicide. And then one day that child might open the paper that says "homosexual elected in San Francisco" and there are two new options. One option is to go to California. Or stay in San Antonio and fight!

Two days after I was elected I got a phone call. The voice was quite young. It was from Altoona, Pennsylvania. And the person said, "Thanks."

And you've got to elect gay people, so that young child and the thousands upon thousands like that child know that there is hope for a better world. Know that there's hope for a better tomorrow. Without hope, not only gays, but those blacks and the Asians. The disabled. The seniors. The Us's. Without hope the Us's give up. I know that you cannot live on hope alone but without it life is not worth living. And you.

And you.

And you. Gotta give them hope. (Reynolds 2019, 288–89)

This quotation is from a speech by the iconic gay politician Harvey Milk. This simple statement had a very early and profound impact on me. It concisely sums up what has been the underpinning of my life and my life's work on behalf of people in society who are "other."

I was in college in the late 1970s and early '80s. I was exposed to a plethora of ways of looking at the world that challenged most of my world perceptions. This confrontation of preconceived notions is what college should vigorously do. However, like most institutions of the time, it did not broach issues of lesbians and gays in any manner. As a young man coming to terms with who I was, I struggled alone: there were no "out" professors or staff members; sadly, I felt that the fledgling gay group on campus were not "good gay" models, and I steered clear of them. Nonetheless, in my junior year I came out to all of my friends and a year later to my parents. The act of coming out was so freeing that I never looked back even though after coming out I received hate messages on my dorm room message board, was called the f-word while walking across campus, and had fire crackers placed under my door in the middle of the night.

So much changed for the better when I went to graduate school in San Francisco. I moved there two-and-a-half years after Harvey Milk, the charismatic member of the city's board of supervisors, was assassinated. After this tragic death, the city burgeoned with gay activism and pride, and as a young gay man, I fully embraced Harvey's message of coming out for the betterment of my community and the larger community as well. My voice professor in graduate school was an unapologetic, proud gay man, and he and his partner were great role models for me. These combined experiences, micro and macro, showed me that there was real hope ahead for me and others and that a life of wholeness and authenticity, plus rights and freedoms my straight peers enjoyed—rights and freedoms that were virtually nonexistent at that time for LGBTQ people in America—were possible. I vowed to never go back in the closet and that I would always be out at work, no matter what that meant for my career, so that my students would always have someone to turn to.

I was extraordinarily fortunate that my first full-time job was in a supportive environment at the very same graduate school from which I had just graduated. Yet even in San Francisco and at a music conservatory, there were closeted faculty and staff. The president of the college at the time was widely rumored to be closeted. Most "knew" that he was gay, and he acknowledged this to me, but he apparently never felt comfortable to acknowledge publicly the fact of who he was. I assume—and if my assumption is correct, I fully understand—that his reluctance to come out was due to the times in which he found himself president (the mid-1960s through the 1980s). Although I understood why he was not out, I remember thinking what an impact he would have had by being out—and what a tragedy for him and for students that he wasn't.

A year after that first job, I moved to New York City to continue my musical studies as an opera singer. Moving to New York after San Francisco was a major jolt to me on many levels. Like San Francisco, New York had many LGBTQ people, but compared to San Francisco, New York seemed very closeted to me; most people were out only in their nonwork lives. This juxtaposition of experiences in these two cities only deepened my convictions to be publicly out, and when I started working at Manhattan School of Music in 1985, I continued be deliberately visible. I was honored by the numbers of students who came to me to talk about being LGBTQ as I was one of a handful of faculty and staff members who were visible. Many of these students later thanked me for being there for them, and a few told me that our talks helped them avoid suicide. These positive experiences spurred me on to do more beyond my own campus. I founded the LGBTQ identity group within the National Association for College Admission Counseling and organized conference sessions on counseling LGBTQ youth at national and state conferences. I also cofounded the renegade gay and lesbian alumni group of my college alma mater.

As I began to apply for academic deanships, I was clear that I would make explicit that I was an openly gay man, and I did so by adding all of my LGBTQ work to my CV. If an institution would not hire someone who was out, this gave them a clear exit from considering my candidacy. If an institution was open to my candidacy, they realized I would be out on the job. Fortunately, I was appointed to the first college deanship to which I applied. My being gay did not appear to in any way bother anyone. My partner, now husband,

and I moved to Chicago, and my time at Roosevelt University was filled with nothing but acceptance. But my work with students who struggled with their personal journeys continued undiminished as it appeared—and unfortunately still does—that many young people, even those in large, progressive cities, still struggle tremendously with their identity.

As easy as it was for me to be secure in my deanship, the opposite was true in realizing a presidency. I was a finalist in five presidential searches. In three of them I found out directly from members of the search committees that the institutions' trustees passed on my candidacy because I was gay. Although knowing this was hurtful, it did not deter me from pressing on, and ultimately I landed in the perfect place for me, Manhattan School of Music. My husband and I live on campus, and we are active in the institution's life. Every year we invite identity groups to our home to demonstrate our support of them as treasured community members. Every time we meet with the LGBTQ students, we ask them when they first knew that I was gay, and every time they cite my student orientation speech, when I tell the assembled crowd that my husband and I live in the residence hall. I then ask them how that made them feel. Their top two answers are "proud" and "safe." So, even in New York City, even in a music conservatory, and even in the twenty-first century, the work of helping others come out and lead lives that are proud, whole, and good continues. So even today, each day, I try to carry the spirit of Harvey Milk with me daily as I continue to do the work in which I so passionately believe.

REFERENCE

Reynolds, A. 2019. *The Children of Harvey Milk: How LGBTQ Politicians Changed the World*. New York: Oxford University Press.

Regina Stanback Stroud

I never came out—I just *was* out. As an African American woman raised in the segregated South, I am intimately familiar with systems of oppression, marginalization, and exclusion. One gets practiced in recognizing and responding to the unjust and hurtful realities of the day. But perhaps my experience as a black woman informed my experience as a woman who loves another woman. In other words, I didn't know to "come out" as a lesbian—like being black, it was just a part of me for any and everyone to see or not.

When I became a college president, I had to consider not only my self-representation, but also how I represented the college, my chancellor, and the board—but to them, that was a non-issue. The bigger question for me became less about what being out meant, but what impact did I want to have on the lives of the people the college served? How would I use my position of influence and consequence to make it even matter that I served as the college president? And, how would I use that role to work on something larger than myself?

I married a man in the US Marines, had a nuclear family, and experienced the American dream with tremendous heterosexual privilege. My former husband and I grew apart and ultimately divorced. During that time of separation, I met a woman. I confided in a friend that I was nervous around her and that "I kind of feel like you feel when you meet a guy that you like." When my friend suggested that maybe I like her like a guy, it was the most unbelievable possibility she could have suggested. Yet, she was right. I was absolutely in love, and I didn't know how to navigate the whole LGBTQ scene.

I didn't identify as a lesbian or as gay or as bi—I was just me . . . and I loved her. I believed that you love whom you love, and their race and gender were incidental. So, there was nothing to come out about—anymore than I came out when I dated a man. I acknowledge the privilege to have that perspective—afforded me by people who suffered. Even so, when I became president, it was important for me to be out so that others who did not enjoy the same ease, facility, acceptance, and support would be able to count on the fact that I had some type of understanding about the experience of being in a same-sex relationship today. As a president and now as a chancellor, my being out is a presentation of myself as a service—a gift. It is a declarative statement of the richness that diversity bestows on an institution. It is a statement to the community that I am here to serve and am not only unapologetic about who I am but am proud of who I am and what I have to offer.

Initially, I had reservations that I hadn't paid my "LGBTQ dues." Many people had struggled and paved the way for me to have the luxury to simply love whom I love. I hadn't earned the title of *lesbian* and felt inauthentic using that term. To this day, neither my wife nor I identify as lesbians. There is plenty to unpack around that, so I am not suggesting that it is the right perspective. If someone Black said to me that they do not identify as Black, my reaction would be visceral: I would question whether that they had self-hatred or lacked the awareness of the majesty from whence they come.

I met my wife when I was nearly 40 years old. I was an established professional woman with a few more resources and an education that gave me options. I lived in one of the more progressive states, and I didn't have to confront a negative, mean, vitriolic, discourse that challenged my humanity daily.

Yet I still needed to tell my siblings, my mother in North Carolina, my very religious grandmother.

My siblings were easy. At no point did I worry that they wouldn't continue to love and support me. My mother and I talked regularly. Sometimes about big things, sometimes small talk like what we were cooking for dinner. One evening, I shared that my husband and I were divorcing. She was saddened but comforting. Then I told her that I was seeing a woman. She got quiet on the other end. I sat in silence for what seemed like minutes but was really just a few seconds. Then she said, "uh-huh; that's not surprising . . . so, what are you cooking for dinner tonight?" And just like that, we resumed our rightful mother-daughter places.

Shifting the discussion to a question about dinner might have been her grab for normalcy. Her question might have been an effort to try to pull me back into the female caretaking role that she spent her life trying to create in me so that a man would want to marry me. I don't know which it was.

Nevertheless, not for a moment did I doubt that she loved and accepted me—even though her chauvinistic perspectives were challenged by my defiant activism and feminism throughout my life. I don't pass judgment about her belief in specific gender-related roles because role clarity is what she relied upon as a black woman in the 1950s, '60s, and '70s as she fought for basic civil rights. In the community, specified gender roles were part of the working, and successful, strategy for combating and overcoming the cruelty of legally sanctioned racism in these United States.

As for my very religious grandmother—I cannot say that I really ever came out. She was approaching her eighties when I started seeing my wife, and I figured that there was no need to rock her world, so I chose not to tell her. I wasn't afraid; to the contrary, I am unapologetic about who I am and whom I love. But I was willing to let her stay in her comfortable reality. The trouble is that it challenged my sense of honesty because she continued to be with us for a long time. She turned 90, then she turned 100! Living independently, talking to me regularly, I was now living with a nearly 25-year-old lie. The whole family was in on it, even my ex-husband. She would ask me how he was, and I would call him and say, please call Grandmother Von so she can hear his voice. He would. Finally, when she was 103, I made the decision: I need to tell her that

I have been divorced for decades and have remarried. I planned a trip to visit her in Washington, DC, but she fell and did not survive before I could get there.

As I reflect on my "non-coming-out" story and my authentic presentation of self, I know that I must intentionally balance the importance of representation with the needs of the institution and the communities I serve. While I live out loud, I do not always lead with the story that I have a wife instead of a husband. I have intersecting identities. How I experience these intersections continues to evolve as I grow professionally and personally, and as my roles and visibility shift. As presidents, chancellors, institutional leaders, we navigate these complex social and political dynamics in service of our own professional lives and the lives of others.

CHAPTER 5

Leading Inclusion on the Campus

As we lead on issues of diversity, inclusion, and equity, one challenge is to ensure that we're not making assumptions about others' experiences of oppression on the basis of our own experiences of oppression. In this chapter, we address our responsibility and experience as LGBTQ leaders in shaping campus culture. We speak to our communities as marginalized people in some ways, but we are privileged in others. Some of us have experiences of being dismissed as self-serving "diversity leaders" when we attempt to lead on diversity; others have struggled with being magnets for diversity concerns when community expectations outstrip our actual expertise. All three authors in this chapter—Regina Stanback Stroud, Erika Endrijonas, and Daniel López—are community college leaders. Each describes realizations about how their LGBTQ identity became an asset to leading campus equity efforts.

Regina Stanback Stroud

When I focus on myself and my own history, my needs, my professional ambitions, it's easy to catalogue the challenges I have faced or the barriers I had to overcome. But when I shift my thinking to the students and the communities we serve, I can call upon my own cultural, social, and professional capital in service of others. At that moment, I feel tremendously powerful, and I experience an amazing sense of comfort with using that power to do good work, to create excellent and inclusive institutions.

While the leadership orthodoxy offers frameworks, theories, and philosophies that are generally grounded in traditional gender and cultural relationships, there has been some research into the leadership approaches and qualities of leaders of color and women leaders. Yet, one would be hard pressed to find literature on whether there are particular traits, strategies, or approaches common to LGBTQ leaders—it's largely an unexplored question.

As I evolved as a leader and gradually assumed roles of increasing responsibility in higher education administration, it never crossed my mind to connect myself as a woman in a same-sex relationship and marriage to the type of leader I would become. My leadership perspective is influenced by my own lived experience. My experiences as an African American woman in these United States prepared me for some of the challenges I would face in leading a historically white institution. I learned customs and habits from my community that helped me navigate some of the direst of circumstances and harshest conditions. Yet, I haven't been conscious of my sexual orientation having that same impact.

As I deepened my leadership skills and scholarship, I theorized a leadership framework that has guided me over my years as president and now chancellor. Called "Leading to Transgress," it is

a theory of leadership—a multi-racial, multicultural identified, gender- influenced framework that is informed by leaders—who are a part of or situated closely to the masses of marginalized people of color—whose primary purpose is to influence allocation of resources in a way that breaks down or transgresses existing systems of power and privilege in the pursuit of social justice. Leading to liberate, strengthen, and educate. Leading to free the oppressed and to change the racist and sexist structures of power and privilege. Leading to develop the depth of humanity and to maximize human potential. Leading to make a difference in this world. (Stanback Stroud 2009, 137)

As an LGBTQ president and chancellor, my leadership is encompassed within this framework—but perhaps has been overshadowed by the intersectionality of my existence. As a person of color, a woman, a professional, a person of relative wealth and privilege (meaning, I do not have to wonder about my shelter, food, health care, or comfort), I simultaneously hold opposing positions, of having power and privilege yet being oppressed and marginalized—or, of being in a leadership position in a system traditionally designed to exclude people like me.

This consciousness presents me with the opportunity to be intentional in my leadership role. That intentionality can lead to greater awareness of the conditions and the needs of students, faculty, and staff. I can pay particular attention to the campus climate for LGBTQ students, faculty, and staff. I can question practices and habits in the institution that fail to create the spaces that support LGBTQ community acceptance and success. I can consider multiple domains of diversity and inclusion. What data are we not collecting? What goals do we set? What are our hiring practices? What curriculum implications are there? How are we communicating to the community? What images do we use to represent the institution? What services do we offer? What admissions processes do we use that may inadvertently exclude or give a message that one is not welcome? What types of people do we honor, celebrate, and glorify? What language are we using?

A few years ago, I had the honor and pleasure of appearing on a long-running show on San Francisco's public radio station KQED, with Michael Krasny. Admittedly star-struck, as I responded to one of his questions, I proudly spoke of the college's programs and services that were grounded in our social justice mission. I mentioned that we targeted students who were historically underrepresented in higher education; I was proud of recognizing that given the emerging demographics, "minority" communities were no longer a "minority" but were indeed minoritized. For all my critical consciousness and racial literacy, I had to be reminded by a listener that I shouldn't "target" people of color, because some of the people we are speaking about are targeted every day in legally sanctioned strategies designed to criminalize, incarcerate, and/or kill them.

The public radio listener's request was one of the clearest examples of how I, as a leader, had the opportunity to challenge my own language and to change the very narrative of our college. It didn't stop there: we demilitarized the language to the extent we knew how. Faculty were no longer in the trenches; we didn't target people; there weren't landmines out there. We weren't combating student issues. We didn't take a shot or shoot for things—and so on. While it might seem semantic or trivial to some, to people whose daily existence includes living with a target on their backs, it's everything. That single experience allowed me the opportunity to change the language of the entire institution. Now that's power.

As presidents of institutions of higher education, that power shouldn't be lost on us. We must be willing to use it to make a difference in people's lives. Yes, that kind of power can have a life-changing impact on a student, a faculty member, a staff member.

The Academic Senate for California Community Colleges established the Regina Stanback Stroud Diversity Award and for more than two decades has given it in my honor to faculty who have made an impact on diversity and inclusion. Yet despite that recognition as a leader in diversity and despite being a critical race scholar with a terminal degree, I got it wrong in front of a national audience. Because none of us are as culturally fluent as we want to be, it is important for all of us, even the most accomplished, to continually learn and grow.

Imagine the pressure, effort, initiative it requires for leaders who just want to do the right thing but are afraid they will say something or do something that is perceived as racist, sexist, homophobic, or elitist. Like the public radio listener did with me, we must give each other permission to be imperfect. Discussions of race, class, gender, sexual orientation, and gender identity are complex, and most of us are not as sophisticated in engaging in them as we would like to be. As eloquent and erudite as we may be as scholars and leaders, when it comes to diversity, many are not. As a leader, I give diversity the respect it deserves, and I treat it as a scholar treats a respected body of knowledge. I read, study, engage, and listen. I do not assume that my expertise comes from my intersecting identities—an African American, educated, professional woman who is married to a woman.

A college president has a considerable amount of power: the capacity to direct and influence things, ideas, people, agendas, events, resources, goals—indeed, the entire direction of the institution. And a willingness to use that power with intentionality is precisely the condition that can create environments which are welcoming and inclusive.

REFERENCE

Stanback Stroud, R. 2009. "Theorizing African American Women's Leadership in Predominantly White Institutions of Higher Education." PhD diss., Mills College. ProQuest order no. 3352309

Erika Endrijonas

Leadership doesn't happen in a vacuum. It's equal parts personal identity, life experience, and a sense of responsibility.

Early into my career, I never thought that my identity as an out lesbian impacted my work as an academic administrator or that it carried with it any additional responsibility. To me, my sexuality was of more interest on a personal level with my colleagues than it was anything else. While some might say that my identity shouldn't impact how I do my job, it's clear to me in hindsight that it's a mistake to separate my identity from my work because it's actually a huge component of my strength as a leader. It allows out LGBTQ leaders like me to clearly see the obligation to create inclusive environments on our campuses.

I haven't always been conscious of this responsibility, though. In my first community college dean position, I oversaw a wide array of career technical education programs, and no one was more surprised than I was to find myself indecisive when faced with a situation that overtly called attention to my identity. A tenure-track faculty member in the administration of justice (AJ) program asked me to arrange a "real crime scene analysis" final exam in the Allied Health Learning Lab. The morning of the final exam arrived, and with it a news crew from a local TV station that had been invited by the AJ faculty member to see this applied approach to a final exam. I wasn't too concerned until the director of the lab came to see me about the news crew filming the crime scene. The AJ instructor had created a rather gruesome scene for the exam that mimicked the infamous Lorena Bobbitt "crime of passion," and it included a severed faux penis lying in a pool of faux blood near a faux male victim. The lab director begged me to come to the lab to view the scene and stop the TV station from filming; as the only out lesbian feminist dean at the college, my mind immediately jumped to how to avoid being filmed inspecting such a spectacle. Would my presence at the exam crime scene be viewed as tacit approval of the pretend dismemberment of a male, given my politics and my sexuality?

I felt paralyzed by a sudden need for self-protection. Instead of marching six hundred feet down the hallway to address the situation, I stayed in my office. Rather than focusing on how I might have been viewed, I should have been more concerned with the extremely negative, needlessly gruesome, potentially offensive, questionable academic exercise.

In my first presidency, over ten years later, the issue of all-gender bathrooms pushed me into another leadership moment defined by my sexual orientation. This time, however, I was ready for it.

In 2016, California passed AB 1732, which requires that in all public facilities, all single-use restrooms be designated "all gender" so that any person who is either gender nonconforming or in transition can use a restroom without having to choose between the binary "male" and "female" options. My campus was a combination of buildings that dated back to the 1960s and some that were just a few years old. In the older buildings, there were a very limited number of single-use restrooms; at least four of the buildings used for many classes only had one single-use restroom, which was locked and designated for staff and faculty use only. These buildings were located next to one another, so any student who wanted to use a gender-neutral restroom had to leave this bloc of buildings in search of a restroom.

With the support of several faculty members, a group of LGBTQ students and their allies figured out the college process for requesting that all single-use, gender-neutral restrooms be unlocked; they went to the committee that handles issues related to use of space and secured a motion that was then forwarded to the college council, which ultimately made recommendations to me as the president.

As this motion was making its way through the shared governance process, the president of the academic senate came to talk to me. A very open-minded person, he was struggling to balance his role as the leader of the faculty and what he thought was the right thing to do. He couched the fundamental conflict as one pitting the faculty against the students, which he wanted to avoid. I agreed that avoiding such conflict would be better, and I asked what the major objection was for faculty. His response was that they were concerned that students were dirty and would probably use the single-use restrooms for sex or drugs.

I was speechless. The faculty demonizing students to retain privilege was a new one for me. It was clear to me that this was, in fact, a fight over privilege: the faculty wanting to retain the privilege of having their own restrooms and students chafing against that privilege. Even more alarmingly, however, it was also clear to me that this characterization of students who would use the restroom had strong undercurrents of sexism and homophobia.

The showdown over this issue came at the college council meeting, where the motion was presented. The students spoke to the issue eloquently. They were having a hard time getting to a restroom between classes, they felt unsafe in the communal bathrooms, and they felt that the situation was taking a toll on both their physical and mental health. The faculty reiterated their assertions about drugs and sex. The senate president was forced to offer a "compromise" voted by the senate that essentially would have required me to make building-by-building decisions about unlocking restrooms based on a "reasonable distance" between them, and I was to be the one to define "reasonable." I could feel the conversation sliding to a point where having some restriction on public accommodations was being defined as reasonable.

I rarely spoke at these meetings because all of the motions passed ultimately came to my desk for a decision. But on this day, I couldn't sit silent. I drew on my background as a historian, and I said that I felt like the discussion harkened back to the debate over public accommodations in the Civil Rights Act of 1964. I then referenced my identity as an out lesbian president, and a faculty member who often referenced her own racial and gender identity muttered to those around her, "Oh, I can't believe she's going there. . . ."

In fact, this was truly the first time I had gone "there" in a controversial situation as the president, and it was, in my opinion, imperative to do so. Of course, I had been out from the beginning, and I attended many events that celebrated the many identities and cultures of our students, including the LGBTQ community, but this was the first time that I had been called upon to support "my people" in a high-profile, negatively charged situation.

The faculty who wanted me to support their privilege probably still think that I only supported the students because of my identity and not because it was the right thing to do. What they don't understand is that my identity was essential in helping me understand what the right thing to do was.

As out LGBTQ leaders, we must always do the right thing, and we must not be afraid to draw on our identities to create and ensure the best, most inclusive environment for the entire college community.

Daniel López, Jr.

I write this essay from the perspective of an immigrant, non-native speaker, former undocumented student, Latinx, and queer man who has had the privilege to study and work at several and very different higher education institutions. I have attended and worked in community colleges, four-year public and private, urban and rural, and predominantly white and Hispanic-Serving Institutions. During my 25-year tenure, I have had the opportunity to be part of diversity and inclusion initiatives at college campuses. I have developed initiatives and made decisions that have made significant contributions to the LGBTQA and other marginalized communities. My approach to addressing issues of diversity and inclusion are based on my lived experiences and my personal intersections of culture, language, race, and sexual orientation. These intersections have helped me to navigate, survive, and thrive in a higher education system that was not meant for people like me, as a student, later as a professional and now as a college leader.

During the early years of my career, my focus was to represent and give voice to the few Latinx students and new professionals in higher education. There, I had the opportunity to be part of and lead a Latinx affinity group that advocated on behalf of Latinx students, faculty, and staff, a community that was almost invisible at this institution. On the contrary, the LGBTQA community was quite visible and engaged at this campus. However, at the time there were very few out leaders. The heavy lifting was conducted by LGBTQA students and allies who often were working in the shadows. Although I was not as engaged in the LGBTQA community at this institution, the skills and experiences I gained would be of great value in serving other marginalized groups including LGBTQA, Latinx, and undocumented communities.

A few years later I was thrilled to join an institution and serve as their multicultural director. Here I was charged with creating an inclusive community for several marginalized groups that included LGBTQA. This was my first formal opportunity to lead campus-wide diversity and inclusion initiatives. As a multicultural affairs director, I was expected to lead sometimes difficult conversations and develop and implement strategies to advance the institution's diversity mission. This institution was clearly ahead of many. Although I felt I had the support of the college leadership, faculty, and students, I did not have the authority to make significant changes to the college. My work consisted primarily of diversity awareness and training; institutional policy was secondary. This is a reason I wanted to become a college president: so that I would have authority to fully serve the college by developing and implementing policies that would positively advance the diversity and inclusion mission of the institution.

The next step in my career brought me to a more diverse institution. While it was diverse in many aspects, it was not as inclusive. However, its diversity allowed me to be an "out" administrator. I felt very comfortable to share my queer identity and display pictures of my partner in my office for the first time in my career. After serving in different capacities, I became the vice president and was charged, among other things, with the institution's diversity initiatives. During my tenure, I led the institution with the creation of a diversity center that successfully advocated for all-gender bathrooms, use of pronouns, and preferred name policy, thereby advancing our goal of becoming a more inclusive campus.

In addition, I also had the opportunity to create services for undocumented students mirrored on the LGBTQA Safe Zone program. These initiatives pegged me as a "self-serving" campus leader for "gay," "undocumented," or "Latinx" leadership but seldom for all. However, I refused to accept this. I often challenged those that felt this way not with words, but with actions. As a member of several communities, I understood the issues, and I was committed to working with the entire college community to earn their support and trust. Although it was at times a heavy burden, I am thankful to those who stood behind me and gave me the space to prove them otherwise. I learned early on in my career that the higher position I had, the more visibility and scrutiny I would encounter. This is why as LGBTQA leaders we must lead and advocate for the entire college community. We must lead by example, with integrity, professionalism, and compassion.

I have known I wanted to become a college president for a while. However, as a Latinx, gay man, and immigrant, I knew it was not going to be easy. I also didn't have a traditional path to the presidency. Although I had experience in academic and student affairs, I was not a full-time faculty member who moved up the academic rank of professor, dean, and provost. To make matters worse, I was a student affairs administrator seen as unprepared for the presidency, an erroneous assumption that I would argue is perhaps the best preparation for the presidency. As a Latinx and immigrant professional, I knew that I had to convince others that my accent and appearance are an asset not a liability. Similarly, as a gay man, I knew I had to convince others to focus on my skills and accomplishments, not on my sexuality. In addition, as queer leaders, campus location is another significant barrier, often limiting us to urban institutions.

It was clear to me that I had much to offer to the presidency. As a queer, Latinx, first-generation, undocumented, and immigrant, I believe that these identities would make me a better president. I not only had many years of experience and a record of accomplishments, but I had the ability to identify with students and their families. I also take very seriously my responsibility to serve as a role model to students and staff, advice that I took to heart from caring professionals of color and queer leaders who supported and mentored me throughout my career.

Although I am relatively new to the presidency, I believe my past career and personal experiences have adequately prepared me to serve in this role. Diversity, inclusion, and equity are and will continue to be at the center of my work. Every decision I make must pass my diversity, inclusion, and equity yardstick. Having the right people on the leadership team who understand and have experience doing true diversity work is crucial. I am committed to having diverse voices on my leadership team, even those that I may not agree with. It is also important to have staff and faculty representation that closely mirrors the students we serve. Having a clear and concise college mission and values that address diversity, inclusion, and equity are of paramount importance. Diversity, inclusion, and equity must also have a prominent place in the college's strategic plan, and equity plan. Furthermore, my actions must go hand in hand with our written statements of diversity, inclusion and equity. I also plan to continue to reach to mentors, individuals, and professional organizations and networks throughout the country for guidance and support—all in an effort to create and maintain a safe, supportive, and equitable campus conducive to learning and personal and professional growth.

CHAPTER 6

Leading in a Heteronormative/ Heterosexist World

How do we experience expectations of conformity and assimilation? We recognize that our roles often inoculate us from many of the effects of oppression, but at the same time our leadership is impacted by minority stress (chronically high levels of stress faced by members of stigmatized minority groups), code switching, and identity policing. How is our queerness perceived or characterized by our constituents, and does that change in moments of transition or crisis? Raymond E. Crossman writes first as a president of an urban private university who considers the effects of heterosexism in higher education and in his own head. Second, Richard J. Helldobler, president of a public university, describes heteronormativity in search processes, the press, and higher education organizations. Finally, Theodora J. Kalikow, retired from a public university presidency, views the construct of heteronormativity somewhat differently—seeing damage as well as opportunity.

Raymond E. Crossman

I first attended the American Council on Education's (ACE) annual meeting in 2004 as a new president. I recall walking into the opening lunch, which was a "presidents-only" event. I was excited. I'd never imagined myself as a member of this community of leaders, and although I was laden with some imposter syndrome baggage, it was undeniable that I was in the room carrying the appropriate credential.

A university president from the ACE board welcomed us with a joke about his school's sports team winning a big game the prior night—as he made eye contact with the president of the losing school's team, who himself shook his fist at his colleague on stage. I don't remember the sport or the universities. I do recall the thunderous and stage-y laughter from the audience of mostly white straight men. I also recall my excitement evaporating and trying to understand why. I'd been in plenty of rooms of white straight men without flinching.

Why was I flinching? It wasn't the odd aspect of two supernerdy scholars beginning an education meeting with a sports reference. It wasn't the creepy factor of two white men mock-fighting about "their" teams. It wasn't the grand gesture of dominance, prestige, and hierarchy. It wasn't even that my own institution didn't have an athletics program. I realized it was that I'd just heard, before the meeting even got underway, the marker of who belongs in the room. And it wasn't me.

Straight men often greet each other with sports references. Gay men and women most often do not. For me, sports were the vehicle for being emotionally and physically bullied in gym class by my classmates, or the soundtrack of unhappy childhood holidays when I felt different and separate from the males in my extended family. But rather than a product of my particular childhood, I believe that I flinched during that lunch because of a design much bigger than me. The meeting opened with a declaration about the conditions for membership in the community of higher education leaders. The flag of structural heterosexism was unfurled on stage, and although

I believe there was no conscious intent to exclude the very few gay men and few women in the room, I understood the rules of inclusion and exclusion right away.

Heterosexism is ubiquitous in a heteronormative world. What is interesting to me is what we make of heterosexism when it occurs in a leadership context. I've been surprised by the missteps I've made and the successes to which I've contributed when faced with heterosexism as a leader.

My response to being slapped at ACE was to make sure that I wasn't excluded: I got myself onto one of the commissions at ACE. But as it turned out, it wasn't a thoughtful or good response on my part. I confess it was a bit of a mess. I never have nothing to say, but in this commission, I had nothing to say. Or rather, I had less to contribute than I would now. I let the initial injury of exclusion turn into a second injury of putting myself in a room for which I was not yet prepared or credentialed—which of course then felt like the original injury. But the latter one stung more.

A few years later in my presidency, a video surfaced online that was apparently made by a student or a former student of our institution. An old World War II movie clip had been reworked to attack me and my institution's administration. Nazi officers speaking in German were subtitled to be handling orders to raise tuition so that the Führer (me) could buy more "shiny purple suits." After the video was noticed online, my colleagues were upset, and they were worried about me. I reassured them that the attack was part of the territory as a leader; I was fine, and I wasn't taking it personally. Then I went home and cried to my partner, "I don't even *have* a purple suit!" I did have shiny suits, I noted through my tears, but I didn't wear them to work.

I was hurt not because I was likened to the Führer, but rather because the attack was crafted in a way that could only be directed at a gay man. I experienced it as a heterosexist attack, disparaging me because I am not heterosexual, rather than as a homophobic attack, targeting me because I am queer. Discrimination rather than hate. A fine line, I know, but for me, psychologically, different buttons are pushed. For me, exclusion elicits shame, sadness, and anger; assault elicits fear and anger.

What did I do? I'm unhappy to admit that I "straightened" my wardrobe up. Prior to this event, I had fun with work clothes. Creative and exuberant dress was part of my expression of my leadership. It was one way for me to "come out" within each interaction, which in the early 2000s was a bit of a political statement and a stand-out from my few peer queer civic leaders in Chicago. Since then, and to this day, I treat my work clothes more as a uniform than I had previously.

I tell myself and others that my tastes changed. I realize there's more to it. There's the effects of heterosexism internalized.

I'm writing about clothing, but I also realize I'm writing about both an indicator and a metaphor for the rest of my deal inside those clothes. How often do I straighten up my leadership? How often do I disregard my superpower of queer intuition, how often do I not reach for the fabulous, and how often do I fail to express queer exuberance and appreciation for fierceness in an idea or behavior?

A few years later, something else happened. I was shopping for suits—choosing black, gray, brown—and I saw a purple swatch. Queer exuberance bubbled up. Yaass—fierce!

My first purple suit was eggplant. My newer purple suit is pansy. Progress. Perhaps the next one will be shiny.

In my new era as a purple suit wearer, my concomitant leadership behavior is to pay attention to heterosexism. I know heterosexism isn't going anywhere, and unfortunately, it's there to stay in my head too. And it can be pretty sneaky, because as is the case in my examples of the ACE breakfast and the subtitled Nazi video, heterosexism doesn't always come clearly labeled as such. One of the wisest mentors I know, when I'm describing a challenge, consistently says, "Consider racism as an explanation." Or sexism, ageism, or the like. So now, when I'm in a twist, or lack compassion for myself, I think, "Consider heterosexism." It stops me from doing things like barging ill-prepared into a commission, and more importantly, I'm more able to lead with a centered mind and heart.

Richard J. Helldobler

Mitch Daniels, president of Purdue University, recently used the term "rare exotic creature" as a descriptor for a highly valued faculty member he was seeking to recruit. With all the talk about diversity and inclusion and yet the lack of recognition of LGBTQIA+ presidents by national organizations, many LGBTQIA+ presidents feel as if we are highly conspicuous and yet still invisible exotic creatures.

We know that the system of higher education in America was developed to educate privileged white men. And because higher education is so slow to change, we shouldn't be surprised that many of our systems continue to privilege straight white men. The presidency, similarly, is not immune from straight white male privilege. In fact, as a gay president, I find that, at times, it can be the most visible job in which one can be simultaneously personally invisible. And we must recognize from the start that the position is still basically structured for straight married folks. Let me relay an experience I had while interviewing for a presidency in western New York.

When an institution is using a search firm, I'm always upfront with the search consultant about my sexuality. I don't want to be surprised, and I certainly don't want a future employer to be surprised during a highly public interview process. When this particular consultant called to say that I was invited for a campus interview, I asked if my partner was welcome to attend. He said, of course, that the visits were scheduled for couples, with some events together and others separate. What struck me about this experience was that, while we planned well, the overt assumption of heterosexism kept surprising us and putting us in awkward positions throughout our visit.

For example, the consultant asked for my partner's résumé so that they could look into employment opportunities for him. My partner works in secondary education, and a meeting was scheduled with the local school district superintendent. It was my partner's first meeting of the two-day interview process. When he walked in, he was greeted by, "Wait a minute, I thought the person interviewing for the presidency was a guy?" My partner replied, "He is." "Oh" was the response. Luckily, my partner is unflappable. Clearly, the presidency is viewed externally as an office for a straight professional couple that fits into common social mores.

We were also careful to check if my partner had to make any public comments or presentations. We were told no, that I would be doing all the public speaking, and his role was to get to know the campus through social settings and by exploring the surrounding community. The search committee scheduled a combined dinner with the college's advisory board, which is akin to the board of trustees, the foundation board, and the alumni group. The dinner was preceded by the requisite cocktail hour, to see how we worked the room. We split up and went in opposite directions so everyone had personal time with both of us prior to dinner.

Just before dinner, the search committee chair suddenly told us that the group would like to hear opening remarks from both of us. As we had been told that my partner would not be asked to make public remarks, I asked if I should speak on behalf of us both. "No," the chair replied, "we want to get a feel for how both of you present publicly." As we sat down, my partner asked me, "What do I say?" My response: "I have no idea, but I'll go second," figuring that would allow for any needed reframing. My partner winged it, saying how much he loved what he saw during the day and how he looked forward to the opportunity to serve as an ambassador for the institution. It was a great, off-the-cuff response, but structuring the evening to see how we presented publicly speaks to the assumption of a "couple" assuming the mantel of leadership, and that the couple they have in mind is a heterosexual couple. It is a sad state that assumptions about gender roles should still be defined in this manner.

Our final event of the two-day interview process was an opportunity for members of the community to meet me and ask questions. Because we were due to leave for the airport right after the meeting, my partner accompanied me. I asked if he should sit up front with me. I was told that he should sit off to the side, but that he would be introduced to the group. Following the introductions, we had a lively conversation about town-gown relations. Toward the end of the session, a man who identified himself as a judge looked right at me, pointed, and said, "I know what *you* are going to do, but what is *he* going to do?" pointing at my partner. My partner looked at me, as if to say, should I answer? I nodded. He reiterated his earlier comments about being an ambassador for the institution and again stated that he was a K–12 educational professional and would be looking for employment opportunities in the area. Had we been a straight couple, our roles would have been easily understood by someone I perceived to be a straight white man. I am grateful to be partnered with one of the kindest people I know, who is extremely smart, good on his feet, and can easily rise above the ignorance of others.

Fast-forward to my current presidency. I was named president and within minutes was doing phone interviews with the local press in northern New Jersey. My first interview went well, lasting for about fifteen minutes. About ten minutes later, the reporter called back. Common wisdom tells you to never take the second call from a reporter, but I was brand new and wanted to establish a good relationship with the press. I answered the phone, and the reporter said, "I've been looking at the boards that you've served on, and many of them are LGBTQA organizations." "Yes," I replied, and stopped. I had learned to make *them* ask the question about my sexual identity. There was a long pause. "Are you gay?" he asked. "Yes," I said. "Is it alright if I put that in the article?" the reporter asked, awkwardly. "If you think it's important," I replied. The headline was, "William Paterson University hires openly gay president."

Many of my William Paterson board members were outraged and wanted to write an op-ed for the local paper in response. I discouraged it, thinking it wouldn't help and that since my sexual identity was now out there, no one should be surprised. But again, if I were a straight white male, none of those descriptors would have mattered, much less become the headline.

Higher education has to own some of this. Some of it, we don't. We need to own that our communities—while committed to diversity and inclusion—don't always demonstrate behaviors or practices that are consistent when dealing with non-"straight white male privilege." We are socialized to believe that leaders are straight white men with subservient wives who work for the institution for free because "it's their job." It's sad that our gender norms allow for such abuse. Here is the part we don't own, and where I am outraged: professional organizations like the American Council on Education, the Association of State Colleges and Universities, and the American Association of College and Universities study the demographics of the presidency and do not count LGBTQIA+ leaders as part of the diversity mix. That sends a dangerous message, and it continues to render an LGBTQIA+ president an exotic creature—one who is highly visible and yet invisible in the larger systems within higher education.

Theodora J. Kalikow

It's 1956, I am 15 years old, and I ask my high school English teacher for a book report suggestion. "Oh," he says, "maybe *The Well of Loneliness*." Never heard of it, but if the teacher recommends it, it must be interesting. I am on a quest! I go to the school library. Not there.

I go to the town library, where I've been going every week since I was 6. I know all the librarians and they know me. My home away from home. Not there. I ask, "Do you have *The Well of Loneliness*?"

Immediately the temperature drops 50 degrees. Gruff, bad looks:

"No—we don't have it." Something is wrong here—they aren't supposed to treat me this way. I have no idea what is wrong, so I carry on:

"It's for a book report. Can you get it for me?" Temperature is now −350 degrees Kelvin.

"No." Her face registers incredulity. I seem to be a liar now, too.

I am in serious trouble but have no idea why. I scurry out of there, very confused. But the quest continues.

I go to my favorite bookstore in the next town. This is where I usually end up when I'm supposed to be shopping for clothes. When I hate all the clothes, I usually get a book. They know me well.

"Do you have. . . . ? It's recommended for a book report."

"No."

"Can you get it for me?"

Great reluctance: "Yes, pay in advance, come back in two weeks." Thank goodness for an established commercial relationship.

In two weeks I come back. They carefully wrap up the book in brown paper and tie it with string. (*That* never happened before.) I unwrap my parcel in the waiting room for the bus.

Oh-ho. Many things become clear. My mind is awash with new concepts. I read feverishly until the tragic end. I tell my teacher I will report on another book. *The Well* lived in the back of my sock drawer until I went to college.

For 60 years I've been wondering why my teacher did that. Over the long run, I have decided that it was a favor. However, I wonder whether he stayed up at night worrying how I would react, and I'll bet he was relieved that I didn't pursue the situation. I wonder how many times he did something like that for some other student? Was he gay himself?

So that was my introduction to heteronormativity and what happens when you transgress the norm. Being a well-brought-up child of the 1950s I didn't do this ever again until I went to college. My tendencies to norm-breaking behavior were all mild enough to be labeled "tomboy." That seemed to be enough to render them acceptable and invisible to everyone except my high school English teacher.

Although this incident woke me up to this particular social norm in a hurry, I soon discovered that most folks don't consciously know it exists: heteronormativity makes most folks blind to us different ones. (Though sometimes we may make them a little uncomfortable.) Oftentimes they just don't *see* us as different unless, of course, we do something really norm-breaking.

And when they do see us, they may see only enough to make them ask tactless questions. "Don't you own any skirts?" asked my favorite mentor one day. "No," I replied, and he didn't pursue the discussion. He came up through Student Affairs, so he heard the clue. The identity police went dormant.

So what does this mean for us as LGBTQ leaders? We have been learning to live with heteronormativity since we were born, or at least, 15. We are all more or less cognizant of the kinds of expectations that our peers or bosses have about things like conformity. My first chancellor, just before he hired me, said, "Of course we know you're a lesbian, just don't be too out front on gay issues." (Actually good advice for a new president in rural New Hampshire or Maine in 1994.)

We can probably figure out what is acceptable behavior for our spouses. Again, this is much more relaxed these days. Some of our never-able-to-be-out predecessors had their significant others "be" the housekeeper or the houseboy/chauffeur.

That is the environment! We don't have a choice; this is where we live. But, in my view this is OK. My observation has been that the heteronormative expectations that almost everybody has can offer a lot of protective coloration for us different ones. Oftentimes they just don't *see* us. Oftentimes we don't see each other, either. Gaydar is fallible and has to be consciously refined. LGBTQ people also have heteronormative thinking.

The gay marriage thing . . . I was sure it wouldn't work. Kudos to GLAAD's Civil Rights Project director, Mary Bonauto, and many others, for figuring out this strategy to win gay marriage. I see it as a successful attempt to throw a part of the mantle of heteronormativity over gay/lesbian couples and families. I wonder if others agree. My thought is that we ought to run with it as far as we can, see which of our other LGBTQ behaviors we could destigmatize or normalize over time. Where will the sticking points be? What would a backlash look like? (Especially these days, there's still a significant segment of the US population that doesn't like Ellen.)

No matter how flaming we may be in personal dress, diction, etc., my bet is that in many other values and behaviors we are pretty much like our straight colleagues: things like academic norms of scholarship, academic freedom, value of the liberal arts, the purposes of higher education, the importance of serving the students, and—yes—the virtues of a balanced budget; there might not be any distance between us. You as leader and change-maker ought to be stressing commonalities so as to get the troops to help with the program you have all decided on. If this is the case, when the crisis comes they are not going to suddenly attack you as a crazed gay person. Actually, in my long experience it is usually the crazed straight people who cause 99.9% of the crises.

Honestly, though, the times have changed so much that I think I alone am alive to tell the tale, but today I think we all are living in a time when heteronormativity is extending its destigmatizing net over a lot more of gay life than before. Perhaps the battles are moving more to transgender and questioning issues. But caution: there can always be backsliding, and there are areas of the country where heteronormativity is alive and well, where expectations for behavior (and punishments for transgression) are as pervasive and rigid as they were in 1956. Here are some opportunities for mentoring—maybe as subtle as suggesting a book report topic. I leave this as an exercise for the reader!

CHAPTER 7

Leading in a Homophobic World

In contrast to the prior chapter, which treated expectations of conformity, this chapter is about experiences of hate. How do past and current experiences of homophobia, even on generally supportive campuses, determine how we lead? What do we do—or are there things we won't do—because of internalized homophobia or because of the real consequences of homophobia? It may or may not be a coincidence that the three writers who are speaking here about homophobia have retired from their roles. Terry L. Allison, a former president of a rural private university, begins this discussion by recounting his navigation of homophobic conditions—highlighting a recent public incident. Karen M. Whitney, emeritus president of a rural public university who continues serving in interim leadership roles, confesses her reluctance to consider the reality of homophobia because such considerations interfere with her narrative of success and how she prefers to lead. Susan Henking, former president of two liberal arts colleges, bristles at the use of the term and then describes how she has worked through homophobic situations, both personally and professionally.

Terry L. Allison

In thinking about how homophobia has shaped my leadership, two quite divergent metaphors came to mind. The first is how homophobia actively suppresses the LGBTQ voice. For some of us gay men, homophobia has meant managing people's hostile reactions to our sounding too queer. Homophobia silences us, making us less likely to lead. I hope that I'm in one of the last generations to experience this phenomenon. My first advice: claim your (gay) voice!

The second metaphor is from Groucho Marx: "I don't want to belong to any club that will have me as a member." As Jewish comedians, the Marx Brothers were rejected by many clubs and therefore objected to the very idea of membership in such organizations. In my case, institutionalized homophobia has affected my willingness to seek out the chummy heterosexist confrerie that still dominates higher education.

Academia is often perceived as a center of political correctness in which every month is Gay Pride, except, of course, at many religion-based institutions that discriminate against LGBTQ students, faculty, and staff as a matter of policy. Even there, the assumption of unquestioned homophobia is fading. But homophobia in higher education runs a wide spectrum, from overt discrimination to more subtle forms of commitment to a heterosexist "good old boys club."

In 1991 I applied for a faculty position at a new campus, Cal State San Marcos, attracted by its multicultural mission. While I soon became a campus symbol of LGBTQ inclusion, I was only able to create change through asserting my voice. Once, while leading a strategic planning session, I heard a conservative faculty member state that the university would harm its reputation by defining multiculturalism to include LGBTQ people. I appreciated the support of my diverse colleagues as I argued for inclusion; at a public university, the academic community was free to assert this value. Those opposing LGBTQ rights had several choices: (a) to continue to speak against LGBTQ inclusion; (b) to work with LGBTQ colleagues and develop more inclusive stances; (c) to move to an institution that shared their belief system. At some faith-based institutions, by contrast, there is no choice; gay voice is silenced, even when it doesn't directly affect teaching and research.

Later, as faculty advisor to a gay-straight student alliance, I assisted when a conservative religious student organization invited the campus to watch *The Homosexual Agenda*, a film that purported to show that the gay movement sought to deprive other groups, particularly people of faith, of their free speech rights. Although students in the gay-straight alliance were upset about the event, I convinced them that (1) the group had every right to show the film; (2) while it may be offensive, we can learn from propaganda directed against us; (3) it was an opportunity to engage with other students about our belief that they are wrong. The audience ultimately consisted solely of officers of the conservative religious club and members of the gay–straight alliance. In a tense situation, our organization fulfilled its mission of confronting homophobia while supporting the mission of exchanging ideas in a safe environment. We had asserted our gay voices and the values of our academic community.

Since those early days, I have lived my academic life as an out gay person. Consequently, as successively dean, provost, and chancellor, I've had to manage community perceptions that I might be a one-dimensional leader interested solely in advancing my own "homosexual agenda." While heterosexuals are rarely perceived to be advancing a heterocentric agenda, we as LGBTQ people are often faced with both overt and subtler forms of critique about privileging our sexual identity.

In 2013, I moved to Indiana to become chancellor at Indiana University (IU) at South Bend. What I found was a state of contradictions. IU enjoyed widespread public and governmental support even within a state that had turned solid red since 2010, with no statewide Democratic office holders and a gerrymandered supermajority in the General Assembly. IU was known for its Kinsey Institute focusing on sex and sexuality, and Blooming-ton has been featured in *Real Queer America: LGBTQ Stories from Red States*. More recently, IU has adopted policies for student rights to use their name and gender of choice while requiring all major con-struction projects to include gender-neutral restrooms. In contrast, Indiana has no statewide antidiscrimination laws that specifically and fully protect LGBTQ people.

In confronting homophobia in Indiana, my most challenging test as chancellor came from the office of the governor and that of IU's central administration. In 2015, then governor Mike Pence was instrumental in the state's passage of the Religious Freedom Resto-ration Act (RFRA), a state law ostensibly about the freedom of reli-gious practice. Although Pence and other GOP leaders denied it, the sponsors' clear agenda was to deny LGBTQ people equal protec-tion. As an out chancellor of a regional campus and a trained aca-demic in queer studies, what opportunities did I have to voice oppo-sition to homophobia?

This is where the Groucho Marx quote kicks in.

Whether you're the president of a private institution given very broad authority by a hands-off board of trustees, or, as in my case, the chancellor of a campus of "one university, multiple campuses" with a centralized administration, you need to consider those authorities' reaction to your public stance against homophobia. My personal lesson involved the trade-offs that the central admin-istration was willing to make in order to preserve the homosocial relationships among the white, straight men who ran the state and the university. Briefly but widely heard, my queer voice soon was silenced to protect those relationships.

Upon the passage of RFRA, I immediately drafted an editorial that criticized the legislation, and I sought permission from the central administration to publish it. The university's president, Michael McRobbie, spoke first, then I followed. Outside the world of higher education, we expect this organizational hierarchy, but people sometimes have the mistaken impression that academic leaders don't experience such a chain of command. After approval, I published an op-ed critical of RFRA in the *South Bend Tribune* that reached thousands of readers.

A faculty member congratulated me on the op-ed and reminded me that the civic backlash to RFRA was itself inspiring. I drafted an article to submit to the *Chronicle of Higher Education* describing how the values of liberal arts education had been successfully deployed in resisting RFRA.* After sending that draft to the central administration for review, I received a condescending email stating that: (1) I couldn't publish a second article, as I'd already made my point; (2) if published, the article would do harm to IU's relationship with the governor during the budget planning process; (3) I was not to worry about my rights, since the legislature was working on a statewide bill to protect them. In sum, I was not allowed to use my position as one of the most prominent gay people in the state (at the time, Pete Buttigieg had not yet come out). Preserving the good old boys club was more important than supporting me as an emerging statewide or national leader confronting homophobia.

My initial reaction was that this group of straight, white guys wouldn't have *dared* to put a similar statement in writing to a woman or person of color, saying in effect, "don't worry, honey; the guys in the legislature will eventually get around to you." But then I checked my sense of privilege, consulting with colleagues before realizing that in order to preserve their heterosexual male homosociality, this group would silence women or people of color. As of 2021, the legislature still hasn't gotten around to us, and I've seen others outside the club sacrificed for an imagined greater good.

---

*As a result of public pressure, including that of major business and university leaders, Senate Bill 50 was enacted in 2015 to prevent certain types of discrimination. The law satisfied many, but not all, critics of Indiana's RFRA.

I respect the IU board of trustees' consistent support of LGBTQ issues. I love that Indiana University has a statewide scholarship aimed at supporting LGBTQ students cut off from family support and an active gay alumni organization. What I didn't love then and don't love now is the suppression of gay voice seeking to confront the pathology of a homophobic governor. A subtler form of homophobia, certainly, but one that still stings.

Karen M. Whitney

Where and when we grow up and begin our careers often shapes us throughout our lives. I grew up and went to college in Houston, Texas. I came of age during the 1970s; I graduated from high school in 1978 and attended the local university that fall. It was a time when you could work your way through college, attend school full time, and still have a rich and busy social life. My high school and college years were bracketed by carefree disco-nights and the repressive so-called Moral Majority. It was a time that was both exciting and terrifying for a woman in her twenties coming out as a lesbian. It was both horribly isolating and incredibly empowering. These were moments and places that continue to influence me today as an educator, administrator, and leader.

Growing up in Texas gave me a thick skin and a tough disposition. The hatred directed at anyone who was LGBTQ was an everyday thing. The quickest way to insult someone's masculinity or femininity was to insinuate that they were "a homosexual." Rumors and gossip (remember: this was before the internet and social media) abounded with accounts of people who got beaten up at school or at a bar for "being a sissy." In the context of my family, hardened rules around gender and expectations of what was "normal" were an everyday challenge. Expectations to date, marry, have children, and conform were nonnegotiable.

When I was a teenager in 1973, the American Psychiatric Association declassified homosexuality as a mental disorder. When I was in high school, Phil Donahue, a widely respected TV talk-show host, devoted a program to homosexuality. I lived with my family in a home with only one TV, and I made sure to watch that show no matter what; I think I held my breath during the entire hour. In 1975, the Houston GLBT Political Caucus opened its doors. In 1978, during my first semester in college, Harvey Milk, the first openly gay man ever elected to political office in the United States, was assassinated. We simply didn't know how to process all this information. Violence against "queers" was commonplace. It was a time when speaking up put you at risk of losing your family, your job, and your life.

While I was in college, things began to change. In 1979, during the summer between my freshman and sophomore years, Houston held its first Gay Pride parade. Four years later I marched in that parade as a volunteer working for the "Gay Switchboard." The Texas Democratic Party added LGBT rights to its platform in 1980. In 1984 the US Supreme Court upheld a decision in *Gay Student Services v. Texas A&M University* that guaranteed LGBTQ college students their First Amendment rights. In 1986, a Texas court case, *Baker v. Wade*, overturned Texas's sodomy laws (a US Supreme Court ruling in *Bowers v. Hardwick* later that year reinstated the law). This was the climate in which I began my career in higher education.

By 1987, I was an area coordinator in student housing. One day the director, who was one of my first awesome mentors, came into my office clearly upset and told me that I had to choose between my job and my live-in girlfriend. I was speechless and just sat and listened as she told me that other staff had spouses or "significant others" living with them on campus. The director explained that "someone higher up" had said that only people who were married could live-in and that "my situation" was immoral. I told the director that my girlfriend wasn't going anywhere and that I would be looking for a new job. Later that year, I became a director of student housing at another university. That wasn't the way I wanted to leave a place and people I loved. It felt like Texas was a state that often took two steps forward and five steps back.

Memories, feelings, and experiences from these events continue to influence how I lead. I am older, and I have successfully held positions of authority and responsibility in higher education. We have made progress. There is still hate, but there is also hope.

Leading in a time of homophobia means that you think about these things and that they influence how you prepare in ways that non-LGBTQ folks can't imagine. For me, this included attending my first homecoming parade with my partner. It was in 2010 in a small rural town where I was a first-year college president. The parade is a huge community event with marching bands, the ROTC, guys riding small bikes, and crowds of alumni, students, and the town's residents. It was also a time when we had to prepare ourselves for possible expressions of hate. My partner and I were invited to ride in an open-air convertible throwing out candy, waving and cheering-on our football team in that typical American college town way. I was in the fourth month of my presidency, and until that point everything had been going well, although my partner and I received a lot of hate mail. As we prepared for this very public event and the possibility of expressions of hatred, we talked through the possi-bilities: would we be yelled at? Or worse: would there be violence? We made plans, and we did our best to be prepared. In the end, our worries were groundless: well-wishers cheered us on, though some looked perplexed as they read the sign on the car that read "Dr. Peggy Apple, Presidential Partner." We *could* have planned for Peggy to stay out of the parade and join me at the stadium or not go to the game at all. But we chose to present ourselves openly as a lesbian presidential couple. We took the day head on and took our rightful place. After all, who doesn't love a good parade?

For almost 40 years I have worked in higher education, includ-ing 20 years at the executive level. I have rarely talked about living and leading during an age of homophobia. Despite my personal and professional accomplishments, was I holding myself back because of the circumstances in which I came of age? To be honest, I don't really *want* to talk about being victimized or marginalized. I like to talk positively—about confidence and courage and all those other things that inspire leaders to meet challenges. Only now, at a late stage in my career, have I considered the consequences of being an out lesbian. The answer, which I guess is obvious, is that coming of age in the 1970s and beginning my career in the early 1980s, had "homophobic consequences," and they informed my story, which, thankfully, is a story of success earned through courage, confidence, and resilience. A takeaway for any leader and for LGBTQ leaders is to proudly be true to who you are, prepare for the worst, and expect the best.

Susan Henking

I admit it. I don't like the term *homophobia*. I was young when it was coined, a portmanteau word that blended the notions of homosexual and fear. (I associate that suffix with fear of open spaces more than anything.) Over the years, I have resisted the ways it medicalizes, psychologizes, and individualizes structural oppression; conflates the experience of gay men with lesbians; risks homogenizing difference; and ignores the ways that lesbians experience the world—or at least how *I* experience it. Using it thoughtlessly excuses or explains rather than changes structural oppression and individualizes what is a systemic problem.

Yet, what many call homophobia has affected me across a lifetime.

Not long after the term came into common usage, I had an experience that continues to shape my understanding of those whose actions might be construed as homophobic in intent or consequence. It is a memory to which I have returned across decades. In the early 1970s, I attended a gathering for the sole purpose of standing up and protesting a speech by the main attraction. The speaker: Anita Bryant. The context: her efforts to repeal laws that had been passed in US municipalities making discrimination against homosexuals in housing and other arenas illegal.

I carry vivid memories of that day—strobe lights flashing against a fading backdrop of long ago.

Picture 1: Walking in, looking "just like them," past police with German Shepherds lining the sidewalks. Though I'm fond of dogs, their presence marked the event as a protest; it recalled those iconic images of civil rights demonstrations in which the dogs' rage seemed egged on by police. I was afraid. It was my first protest. I was barely out. As I walked between the dogs, I wondered whether they would bite me. (I later learned that they were protecting protesters.)

Picture 2: As Bryant said the word *homosexual*, a large group of us, scattered across the stadium, turned our backs and started to leave. I walked down an aisle toward the stairs, while men and women, mostly old and white, screamed and spat at us. I'm now older than they were, but I still remember it the same way: these were people who looked just like me. But they no longer saw me, though they had seen me moments before as I passed among them.

Those moments were a lived experience of radical sameness and radical rejection: for them, I was—we were—not human. Their faces, distorted with anger, fear, and viciousness, remain in my memory.

It was those faces that defined my future political engagement, and eventually my teaching and leadership. I carried them with me as a challenge and an inspiration. Those people were spitting at me *for one reason only*. Not because I was a young white woman—experiencing sexism or misogyny—but because I was calling out the powerful forces of religious homophobia. I learned during those moments that in some circumstances I could pass, while in others I couldn't, and I came to see my whiteness and my age in a new way.

Those moments shaped my career as a teacher and a scholar focused on religion and LGBTQ matters. I studied the ways that, within and beyond the heterosexual mainstream, structures drive us toward homogeneity and conformity. Conformity doesn't protect anyone from anything. Over time, as teacher, scholar, and citizen, I thoroughly embraced the relationship between experience and expertise. I was shaped by the poet Adrienne Rich's 1980 essay "Compulsory Heterosexuality and Lesbian Existence," debates about the imperative to come out, and by coediting *Que(e)rying Religion: A Critical Anthology* with Gary David Comstock. I was shaped by the paradox of students who refused to read about a gay synagogue "because I am not Jewish," while insisting that others who were not LGBTQ read about them. I struggled with the deployment of homophobia as a form of identity politics.

I was also shaped and moved by surprising moments of connection when allies joined me in resisting the realities of heterosexism and homophobia.

Even when I added "leader" to my sense of self and my vocation, the memories of decades ago persisted, reinforced by additional reflections, rooted in political and friendship circles and, most importantly, my relationship with my partner. These provided me a lens through which to experience headlines reading "Lesbian Appointed President of Shimer College," words that made me proud and, though it's hard to admit, embarrassed. As proud as I was, I couldn't forget the reality that people "just like me" had once spat on me. Across a lifetime, the call to conform—and to be different—have remained fruitful, fraught, and haunting. Just as every death reminds us powerfully of earlier experiences of mourning, each experience of homophobia—and of hope—brings back memories of earlier experiences.

During my first year as college president, I visited with a supporter of the college I was leading. As we grew increasingly comfortable with one another, I was shocked when she abruptly said, "I don't agree with your lifestyle." Without any preparation, I replied, "I don't believe in yours either." She responded, "I don't have one," I replied, "Aren't you Catholic?" We debated the meaning of "lifestyle" (a term I hadn't heard in years), and we came to respect one another. I learned that she had been advocate for providing health insurance to partners of LGBTQ employees and, later, that she was an ardent supporter of my own rights. We agreed on the rights of individuals, the centrality of education, the merits of listening, and the power of healthy and strong disagreement. We agreed on one another's humanity. We disagreed—and continue to disagree—on the breadth of what counts as a "lifestyle," the acceptability of being a lesbian, and more.

I have worried in recent years about the thoughtless deployment of the notion of trans-exclusionary radical feminist, how some of us label the behavior of others homophobic in a knee-jerk fashion, and the erasure of lesbians in too many arenas. I've wondered whether policing individual behaviors inhibits the structural change we need.

As I've worked and lived, I've wrestled with the ways that restorative justice can be crucial, the relevance of educative versus punitive responses to injustice, and more.

I believe that to lead is to learn, and that there is value in struggling in public rather than hiding. There can be costs—especially for a white woman of a certain age—to conflating the personal and the professional, but the costs of disconnection are much more serious. I know that we must collaborate, and I know that it isn't easy. I have lived with and through moments of victory and of backlash for lesbians and for women. I have lived and worked alongside a partner whose sense of justice inspires me. During each and every moment, my leadership has been about fear and hope. And, of course, it is about more than the role, though it is also shaped by the roles we fulfill.

Just as importantly, I have been unexpectedly filled with joy in meeting lesbian and gay men presidents and chancellors. The sense of not being alone has moved me deeply. I have wrestled with them to think through the ways a focus on our sameness risks sidelining lesbian voices and others. As I stood among them when marriage equality was announced, troubled by the call to conformity implicit in such victories, I was moved to remember that struggling together can change the world. That moment of fear decades ago, which began as a cautious effort to respond to Anita Bryant, continues to shape me as we seek to bend the arc of history toward justice.

CHAPTER 8

Mentorship

Queer presidents often describe what mentorship was present, important, missing, or disempowering to us as LGBTQ leaders in our journeys to our contemporary work. Some of us never imagined or aspired to a college or university presidency, in part because there was no roadmap for LGBTQ leaders. How did it get from off-the-table to a possible or realistic consideration? The first contributor, Theodora J. Kalikow, is a retired president of a public university who traces her steps from early childhood experiences of being mentored to her current work as the most senior and accomplished mentor in our group. The second author, Richard J. Helldobler, in his second presidency at a public university, describes explicit and implicit mentoring, as well as our responsibility to address the declining number of people interested in higher education presidencies. Terry L. Allison, a retired president of a public university, is the third contributor in this group, and he lays out a framework for "queering" mentorship.

Theodora J. Kalikow

I love mentoring. As a child, before I knew what it was, I had the benefit of several mentors among relatives, camp counselors, and teachers. Some deliberately took me in hand, especially at camp; some didn't particularly focus on me (except as one of a class, for example), but they all demonstrated how to be or what to avoid becoming. My Hebrew school teacher, Simon Young, was a poignant example to me of a scholar displaced by circumstances—the

Nazi regime—into a life of teaching Hebrew to privileged little American brats who mostly didn't want to learn it. Stoic fortitude and high scholarly standards, thy name was Mr. Young.

I had more exposures to mentoring in college and after, by both lesbian and straight mentors. In college, I was fortunate to be mentored by Cary Clasz, professor of speech and theater, who made it her business to refine my Massachusetts North Shore patois into something more intelligible, who encouraged me to take responsibility for much of the backstage theater crew, and who invited me into her home, which she shared with her woman partner. No lectures about being lesbian or gay; just a demonstration that a happy life was attainable.

After college, I was similarly fortunate in my boss at the hospital chemistry lab where I worked for two years before going on to graduate school. Barbara Jones and her partner, Jean Henley, MD, were my "lesbian parents" until they died many years later. They helped me with relationships, cars, and houses; we shared vacation adventures, sailing mishaps, and all things Maine. I wrote my dissertation in their garage in Maine, which they had kindly fitted out with a bedroom and study area so that I could avoid their cats.

A third mentor was Lura Shaffner Teeter, department chair of philosophy for my first teaching job at Southeastern Massachusetts University. Not only did she ease me into the weird world of academe and happily lend me every book ever written about anything I wanted to know; we shared an office, and I watched her wheel and deal at the highest levels of Massachusetts politics for several years, until she managed to get enough new trustees appointed to the board so they could fire our awful president.

The successor to that president became my fourth mentor. Donald E. Walker asked me to be his assistant around 1980. Thus began my adventure in academic administration. As a sociologist and an ordained minister, Don Walker was a master at understanding and directing groups. Often he would tell me what was going to happen at a meeting before it happened. I am grateful to him for choosing me, a person very different from himself in many ways.

My formal introduction to mentoring and its professional implications came from a national organization, the American Council on Education (ACE). In fact, as I think about it, I am glad to acknowledge ACE for its benevolent presence during my entire career in academic administration, as sponsor of the ACE/National Identification Program, the ACE Fellows Program, the ACE Commission on the Status of Women, on which I served, numerous statewide mentorship programs that I led with colleagues, and finally now in appointing me as a mentor and advisor to current ACE Fellows. ACE has always been generous is extending mentorship opportunities to gay and straight colleagues, colleagues of color, those serving two-year and four-year institutions, and international colleagues.

In the 1970s ACE organized the National Identification Program for future women leaders in New England. This was a series of workshops for women across all of higher education that sought to motivate and groom us for leadership roles like department chair and dean. Following this example, a number of us in public higher education designed a similar workshop for women in Massachusetts public colleges and universities, which is still operating. For a relatively junior faculty member like me, it was a great networking and learning experience that connected me to a whole cadre of straight and gay women who went on to have remarkable careers in higher education.

And when I moved to Colorado in 1983, ACE connected me with Brangwyn Foote at the University of Colorado, so we could organize a similar, and ongoing, program for public and private institutions in the state.

From my first exposure to this kind of group mentoring and networking, I was captivated by the kind of learning it provided—a model very different from the individual-centered higher education process that I had recently been through. It depended on a group of women (gay, straight, from private and public institutions, two-year and four-year colleges, majority and underrepresented universities) to bring their experience and perspectives in service of problem solving or other tasks. We each had things to contribute, and we each took what we needed from the process; a surprising feature was the breadth of different perspectives on any situation. I learned a tremendous amount from the peer mentoring/networking format, and I have been doing various forms of mentoring and workshopping ever since. (I learned especially from an early foray into this kind of presentation where the group critiqued the case itself [and its author] more than they tried to grapple with the questions I had posed.)

LGBTQ Presidents in Higher Education is the latest venture. Given the wide range of people answering to this label, and their variations in age and stage, I would imagine that the group/peer mentoring model will continue to work well.

One especially useful feature of the group approach to setting up mentoring experiences is that you can design a general "generative" format and be pretty confident that the participants will benefit from it. The fact that the Massachusetts and Colorado organizations are still operating 35 or 40 years after we started them indicates that the format and the questions are still relevant and important to participants. (Of course, it also suggests that the level playing field in higher education for women, people of color, or LGBTQ colleagues is still aspirational.) Indeed, when I was in Colorado last year I met several recent participants in the program, and they all credited it with motivating them to pursue careers in higher education administration.

Individual mentoring experiences present their own set of challenges. Choosing and being a mentor/mentee; what sort of advice you give and how it is received; how long the relationship lasts; the moral dimensions of the mentor/mentee connection are only some of the issues to be considered. Each of these has an LGBTQ connection that should be explored further.

Richard J. Helldobler

I would preface this essay by observing that I have found mentoring to be both unintentional and intentional. Living authentically as an open LGBTQIA+ person or developing a professional mentor/mentee relationship can positively affect lives and careers. The former was surprising to me; the latter was professionally life-changing.

Early in my career, I lived openly in a long-term relationship while I served on the faculty of a university in southwestern rural Pennsylvania. My doctorate in theater situated me in an artistic community that by and large was welcoming and accepting. That wasn't always the case outside the department, and those moments hit harder, I suspect, because they were such a contrast to my usual day-to-day affirming work life. Yet on reflection, and through time, I have come to understand what my presence or my unintentional mentoring did for many of my students, both straight and gay.

I remember when gay marriage finally became the law of the land in 2015. On Facebook, I commented, "I never thought I would live long enough to see gay marriage." The first student to respond was a straight male who replied that it was through watching me and my partner that he grew to understand gay relationships and came to realize that they were fundamentally the same as those of their straight counterparts. He wasn't taught to be accepting, nor was he exposed to gay relationships prior to college, but our authenticity in who we were helped him understand, accept, and become an ally. Another former student who identifies as gay told me that he had found his mate and decided to marry. I wished him a happy life through social media, and he replied that while in college, he was tortured at the thought of a life as a single, lonely, disease-ridden gay man depicted in much of AIDS-related theater composed during the pandemic. The fact that he and I could talk openly about these issues and that my adult gay life with my partner was so distant from the images portrayed in much of society sent a message to him that not everyone ended up dead and alone.

Years later, I read another social media post whose author remarked that gay male teachers often helped provide a context for many gay male dancers to understand their feelings and emotions while coming out. One of my first dance students was a student from India, who told me that I was the first person with whom he could comfortably discuss his sexuality and that I was instrumental in his path to acceptance.

What was surprising about these unintended mentoring situations was that I had no idea they were occurring. But my living an open, authentic life as a gay male was important for my students, both gay and straight, and well into my late career, the thought of that is heartwarming for me. Now, as a university president, I am mindful of the power of students, faculty, and staff seeing their lives mirrored in the institution. Whether the mentoring is intentional or unintentional, our mere presence can be a powerful tool in reshaping social norms grounded in heterosexism and white male privilege.

As for those who mentored me, I have found that women in positions of power are more likely than men to extend mentoring and career opportunities to openly gay men. Whether that's due to challenges they faced during their careers or to an innate ability to understand that "different" thinking can still be "good" thinking, I have found them more willing than men to expand the circle and pass the leadership torch. This in turn has taught me to think intentionally about mentoring women. Because higher education in general is so steeped in heterosexism, mentoring is not often enough; you have to provide opportunities.

When I was promoted from interim dean to dean, I inherited a group of elderly white male department chairs who basically ran the college. It was clear to me that there was talent within the college that extended beyond this traditional demographic, but because these were elected positions, it wasn't enough to simply mentor women and people of color in academic leadership; I had to find ways in which they could demonstrate their abilities. I enlisted these talented individuals in special projects that they could lead or help drive, which built a case for their leadership within the college. When I left the deanship five years later, a third of the college leaders were women or a people of color.

I remember the day I showed up for my interview for an American Council on Education fellowship like it was yesterday. In my application, speaking to the diversity that I might add to the class as an openly gay man, I expressed concerns that the presidency of a college might not be open to me. The director of the program at the time took me aside even before I interviewed and said words to the effect of "while not impossible, it will be difficult for you to become a president; most boards of trustees will not hire you. But there is one openly gay president out there, and his name is Chuck Middleton at Roosevelt University." During the selection process, I tried to get my placement at Roosevelt, but it was a tough budget year, and Chuck couldn't support the cost of a fellow. But I got myself invited to shadow Chuck during a week when the board was meeting. That week was professionally life-changing for me, I began to understand the power of true mentorship and never looked back. It was clear from that week that I had found a mentor; Chuck didn't know it yet, but I did. After that week, I tried to get 30 minutes with Chuck every time I was in Chicago or when we were at a professional meeting together. And every time, he said "yes." Those 30-minute sessions became longer, as I refined my questions or as the campus issues I was facing became more complex. My mentoring experience with Chuck helped me understand how to position myself as an openly gay candidate in presidential searches and how to answer those questions where sexual identity can do you in if you aren't careful or if the campus is truly not ready for leadership outside of the heterosexism spectrum. I often tell students: Not one of all the people I've talked with has ever said that a smartphone, a computer, or PX90 changed their lives; it was always a person, mentor, professor, staff member, or experience. Chuck certainly is one of the people for me, and for many of the LGTBQ presidents who followed him through the closet door that he opened. And now as a university president I have been intentional in paying it forward.

To my presidential colleagues: we need to talk more about the joys of these jobs. They're challenging, yes, but they're also amazing in so many ways. The next generation of leaders is—trust me—watching and listening. We need to be mindful of the job's challenges, but also more open about the joys. Stephen Sondheim's lyric says, "Careful the things you say; children will listen." And while not children, if we are messaging more about the challenges than the joys to those we mentor, we must own our responsibility for the shrinking pipeline of potential university leaders.

Terry L. Allison

There is no lack of research related to mentoring college students who are questioning, who are coming out, or who want to develop their leadership skills. Kristen Renn provides a concise but extensive overview of best practices in developing an inclusive environment for students (Renn 2017). In contrast, as LGBTQ Presidents in Higher Education found when we were organizing our first leadership institutes, there is little research about LGBTQ higher education leaders. This is in part because until recently there have been few out presidents and chancellors.

So I asked myself, given my experience in being mentored or in mentoring, is there anything distinctively queer about it? If I thought about "queer" as a verb, what could it mean to queer the process of mentorship? In responding to these questions, I join my colleagues in fulfilling a key purpose of this volume: to report on our practices as LGBTQ leaders, which in turn may inform future research, critique, and improvement of our leadership and mentoring.

Queering mentorship in higher education means four things to me:

1. making mentorship available to LGBTQ people in higher education;
2. breaking down the binary of gay-gay or lesbian-lesbian mentorship, but not eliminating it;
3. providing intentional mentorship to those underrepresented in higher education leadership while offering it to all whom we could effectively mentor; and
4. addressing the hierarchies inherent in the mentor/mentee relationship while cultivating the mentor/mentee relationship as one of mutual benefit.

During the 1990s and 2000s, as I matured as a faculty leader, I spoke with some higher education administrators who had never considered the barriers that a single gay men aspiring to a presidency might face: the lack of role models; the unique social status of being "out" in US society; and institutionalized or internalized homophobia. They hadn't thought about how the social construction of "queer predators" might influence a decision to hire someone to lead an academic community of young, developing persons. Queering mentorship in higher education initially meant educating non-LGBTQ leaders about specific conditions, needs, and concerns of LGBTQ people on a leadership path.

Eventually my experience helped in establishing formal efforts to mentor aspiring LGBTQ leaders. I joined colleagues in planning and organizing the first institutes designed specifically for LGBTQ administrators, faculty, and staff with aspirations to lead in higher education. Our goal was to help leaders better understand the search process for senior positions in higher education; what issues might arise for partnered or single LGBTQ senior administrators; to examine areas of practice, such as philanthropy, that might present specific challenges or opportunities for LGBTQ leaders; and to understand multiple aspects of queer leadership.

We tried to match potential mentors and mentees, but even if few formal mentorship relationships developed, we were able to foster connections, increasing the likelihood that LGBTQ aspirants to greater leadership roles would find a mentor. In some cases, we learned that feedback from these relationships helped individuals find their next leadership role.

When one speaks of "queering" something, breaking down binaries is one of the most important tropes that comes to mind. The presumed binary relationship here might be LGBTQ versus straight, dividing those whom one may choose to mentor. To me, queering mentorship in higher education means that even while recognizing the need and the potential benefits of mentoring someone with the same sexual identity, we should not limit ourselves exclusively to any group.

I've had significant female and male mentors, and I've seen many successful mentorships in higher education administration across gender. My most significant mentor, Alexander Gonzalez, was a Latino male president who became known within the California state university system and nationally for helping to foster the academic careers of other Latinos. Recognizing my potential and my needs, he provided me with multiple opportunities to lead on our campus, in our system, and in the community. Without his support, I wouldn't have attained my dean, provost, or chancellor positions. In turn, partly by chance and partly by intention, I've served as formal or informal mentor to several African American women, none part of the LGBTQ community. One aspiring leader was assigned to me, one sought me out, and one I hired.

These relationships developed out of trust and affinity, and partly because I was intentional in trying to achieve greater diversity in higher education leadership, particularly for those with feminist leadership styles. My multiple identities—a white male from the working class who had been bullied for seeming too queer— have influenced my outreach to potential mentees and provided long-lasting relationships of mutual respect and learning. In contrast, one of my attempts to mentor within the LGBTQ community was not as successful as I would have wished. That individual never developed the level of trust or belief in my leadership that was necessary for me to be a successful mentor to him. Recognizing the need for queer mentorship and sharing membership within a community of gay men did not magically make us a good partnership. If I "queered" mentorship in that case, it was in persisting to gently assist without demanding that the individual become my acolyte.

I have queered mentoring by serving as a mentor to white, straight men, providing them with wider perspectives on the queer and feminist values that I bring to the academy. I have mentored men and women who are active in religious organizations that oppose LGBTQ rights or recognition. As a campus leader, I have been in formal mentorship roles with conservative students who, though unfailingly polite, support policy and politicians opposed to full inclusion of LGBTQ people. Without endorsing their beliefs, l provided guidance about creating environments of inclusion. Mentors don't expect to immediately change the positions that a mentee acquired over a lifetime, although we can counsel them about the short- and long-term consequences of adopting specific stances. In queering mentorship, I have demonstrated how to foster space for civil dialogue and to accept differences. For some, my practice has provided contrary evidence to the presumptions of forced liberal indoctrination in higher education.

While queering loves to attack binaries, it also loves to dissolve hierarchies. Adopting true humility in the servant-leader model queers a mentoring role that otherwise might risk becoming patriarchal and patronizing. Recognizing that mentoring is a mutual relationship and that I as mentor can learn as much from the mentee as she or her learns from me have been critical to my approach. I have seen the avuncular sage model throughout my career, but I don't have it in me to play that role. This doesn't mean that as a white male, I never have to check myself if I push my experience as universally relevant. When successful, I reposition my story as an invitation to explore the mentee's experience rather than as a defining model. Queering mentorship has meant that I am aware of the social constructs related to my age, race, gender, and experience and explore with my mentees how they might solve problems effectively given their own experiences. Sometimes my work adds to their understanding; at other times, I have learned a better approach from a mentee.

Recognizing the specific needs of LGBTQ individuals in higher education who seek leadership mentoring is a unique element of queering mentorship. The second two points, breaking down the queer/straight binary and dissolving hierarchies, are not. The combination of the three, however, may constitute a practice of queering mentorship that can contribute to effective leadership in higher education in the United States.

REFERENCE

Renn, K. 2017. LGBTQ Students on Campus: Issues and Opportunities for Higher Education Leaders. *Higher Education Today* (blog). https://www .higheredtoday.org/2017/04/10/lgbtq-students-higher-education/.

CHAPTER 9

Self-Care

As leaders who come from a population that has been historically disadvantaged, what do we need? Do some of us have a hard time addressing our personal human needs because of internalized heterosexism or homophobia (the "best little boy [*sic*] in the world" hypothesis or imposter syndrome)? Or are we focused on self-care because we, as marginalized people, are more open and vulnerable or because we feel more compelled to seek and use support? The first two contributors—James Gandre, president of an urban music conservatory, and Katherine Hancock Ragsdale, the former leader of a divinity school—describe personal and structural barriers to self-care and how leaders might negotiate these barriers. The third author, Theodora J. Kalikow, is a retired president of a public university who writes more generally about the necessity of self-care, with a coda in her essay about its relationship to being out.

James Gandre

Confession: The idea of self-care has always been a difficult one for me: I have struggled with work addiction throughout my adult life. My need to fulfill all my ideas and possible projects, and to care for others at my own expense, whether they be my institutional community, my friends, or my husband, sometimes seems endless. As I often say, I want to stuff twelve pounds into a ten-pound bag on a regular basis. That being said, since my college days I have made steady progress toward a place where self-care plays a larger role in my life. Those who work with me may be surprised to hear that I spend now more time away from work today than I ever did previously. But before we discuss the present, I want to go back to my early adult life.

Being a child of two parents who were generous, kind, loving, wonderful people but who didn't have an understanding about self-care, I think I come by my work habits honestly. My parents were, like me, more likely to look after others than themselves, and they loved to work—a lot. In addition to my in-home conditioning, knowing that I was "different" from the age of 5 or so and, later, understanding what that difference might mean turbocharged my need to be perfect, to be the best little boy—and later the best young man—in the world. I needed to create a protective shield around myself that was reinforced with thick layers of earned and retained good deeds and goodwill in case someone might find out my terrible secret. I hoped that this shield would be my saving grace—that it would preserve me from being disowned or cast out, either from my family, from my small circle of friends, or from my schools. During my youth and young adulthood, I was obsessed with being the best person I could be, and I sought to achieve as much as I possibly could in order to compensate for my secret.

Once I came out in college, I began the process of shedding the need to be perfect: I took the first step toward self-care. In 1979, coming out certainly was not a "good" act in the sense that most people would have defined it. But for me, coming out was an honest, liberating, and empowering act of both defiance and self-care. I was no longer hiding who I was from the world, and I was stepping forward in a more authentic manner. It wasn't an easy road at first. I regularly found hate messages pinned on my dorm room message board; several times, I was woken up in the middle of the night by firecrackers placed under the door to my room.

But I was actually fortunate to have come out earlier than most of my contemporaries, and for the most part my coming out was not the colossally traumatic act that it was for many of my generation.

After college, I attended graduate school in San Francisco, and my world was opened to a new way of living as a gay person, in which I could envision a future of pride and dignity that might offer more opportunities to me and my generation than had been available to earlier ones.

Taking this next step toward not only being honest about who I was, but embracing and loving who I was, was an important part of taking better care of myself. But although I was nurturing my gay self in many good and positive ways, after graduate school I started down my path of work addiction: I was working a full-time administrative job plus two part-time performance jobs. And, in my mid-twenties, after moving to New York, work became all-consuming. In my mid-thirties, I realized something was wrong and sought out a therapist for the first time after reading a wonderful and helpful book by Diane Fassel titled *Working Ourselves to Death: The High Cost of Workaholism and the Rewards of Recovery* and later Bryan E. Robinson's *Chained to the Desk: A Guidebook for Workaholics, Their Partners and Children, and the Clinicians Who Treat Them.* It was at this time that I began going to the gym and trying to take a bit more time out of my week to see a movie or go out to dinner with friends. A few years later, I met the person who would become my life partner and, 15 years after that, when it was legal, my husband.

Having someone in my life whom I cherish and adore was powerful in pulling me toward something other than my work, and that has remained so.

For a while it seemed to me that my newly found awareness of my work challenges and my new relationship had me on a path to ultimately being "cured." My husband and I moved to Chicago when I assumed the deanship of the Chicago College of Performing Arts and left a position that I'd had for ten years. The opportunities and challenges of my new job propelled me backward in my process of dealing with work addiction. When I was appointed provost of my institution, I once again took a breath now and then, and I began to take some time for myself, since there were far fewer evening obligations than when I was a performing arts dean.

Being a president offers a never-ending array of possibilities for over-work, especially during this particular moment, when there are so many assaults on higher education from so many different places. During the first year of my presidency at Manhattan School of Music, a fellow president told me "Make sure to take one hour a day, one day a week, one weekend a month, and one month a year for yourself." That sounded like wise counsel, but during my first years as president, putting that advice into action was elusive.

Between the work of advancing my institution's mission and the myriad events, performances, and dinners that I'm expected to attend each year as a president of a performing arts college, I began to feel that there weren't enough hours in the day to accomplish all that needed to be done. So in my current position, I have to fight my impulse to work endlessly. Between morning walks, exercising with a trainer, watching TV with my husband as we wind down our workdays, I try to take an hour or two for myself almost every day. I take two vacations of two weeks each annually and punctuate the rest of the year with a few long-weekend getaways. I have yet to get close to regularly taking one day a weekend off, but I'm working toward that goal. I'm fortunate to have a wonderful, large terrace on which I do gardening, and that's yet another form of self-care. Gardening and getting my hands into the soil are therapeutic and calming for me: I take pleasure in planting seeds, watching them grow and thrive, and seeing others share in the joy my garden brings me.

My journey of self-care is ongoing, though sometimes it's two steps forward and one step back, but the journey continues, and it continues to progress toward a healthier and more rounded life.

Katherine Hancock Ragsdale

Most of us of a certain age can remember when self-care was considered a form of self-indulgence. Who had time for that? Certainly no one in any marginalized community could afford it. We had to overcome discrimination in order to succeed and, once we had succeeded, we had to excel at everything we touched—to prove that the discrimination was unjustified and to pave the way for those who followed. We high achievers had work to do, dragons to slay; we had no time for bubble-baths or long walks in the park. Our energy was spent on the job; we had none left to burn off in the gym.

Now, of course, we know, and the science has shown, that we had it all wrong. We've learned that not only is unmanaged stress likely to send us to an early grave; it also compromises the quality of our work while we're still alive. Our bodies lose stamina; we can't work as hard or as long as we once did.

Worse still, our brains don't function as well. We don't think as quickly or as clearly. And we lose the ability to see the big picture—an ability central to effective leadership.

Aspiring pilots are taught to develop the habit of scanning each of the cockpit instruments in a pattern that they repeat until it becomes a reflex. Why? Because in times of crisis or high stress, the human eye and mind hyper-focus. Our focus narrows, we lose our peripheral vision and awareness. We put ourselves at serious risk of missing important information; we lose the big picture. On top of that, in the midst of stress, we tend to breathe more shallowly, so our brains get less oxygen—and work less well.

A stressed-out body and mind—whether from the acute stress of mid-air engine trouble or the chronic stress of the unrelenting grind of long days, tough challenges, and one blasted crisis after another—a stressed-out body and mind just don't operate at the highest level of competence So it's in the best interest of the institutions and the people we serve for us to exercise enough self-care to ensure that our bodies and minds are operating at peak performance and able to manage the multitude of daily stressors we encounter. In fact, it's in the institution's best interest for *everyone* who works there also to make self-care a priority so that they can bring their best selves to the table. And we know that they'll be hesitant to do that unless and until they can see that their leaders support those priorities. So our own self-care is not only good for us; it also serves as an example that is good for our staff—both of which are good for our institutions.

Even more far-reaching and central to the quality of the life and work of our institutions is the *presence* we bring into the office and onto the campus. More than we can fully comprehend (which is, perhaps, good—for keeping both our egos and our stress levels in check), we create the climate of our institutions. Others take their lead from us: attempting to follow our example, yes; moving with caution if we're known to be temperamental or when even the most nonthreatening of us is visibly grumpy, yes; but there's also an intangible way in which leaders create the very climate of a place—the air everyone breathes, the emotional field in which everyone moves.

Family systems therapists and clergy have long understood the importance of what Murray Bowen and Edwin Friedman called *non-anxious presence* as a core component of leadership. The term and concept have begun to migrate into understandings of business and organizational leadership, as well. Simply put: a leader who can maintain a non-anxious presence in a highly anxious, charged organization or situation will defuse that anxiety and stress—creating space for everyone to bring their most creative, thoughtful selves into the system and situation. A leader who takes the time to keep his or her own stress in check, to be sufficiently grounded, will reduce the stress and improve the performance of the institution and most everyone in it.

So what does stress-busting, anxiety-eliminating, life and performance-enhancing self-care look like? And what does it have to do with LGBTQ leadership in particular? Self-care is individual. It's universally important, but its design will be specific to the individual and their circumstances. It should be noted, though, that LGBTQ people, like women, people of color, immigrants, and people who are perceived as having disabilities, not only have generally had to battle discrimination in order to achieve professional success but also often feel the need to show no vulnerability, to overachieve, to admit to no needs of any kind in order to demonstrate that the discrimination we faced, and often still face, is unjustifiable.

Escape from unrelenting stress is further complicated because home, which can be, for many, a haven from stress, is often, for LGBTQ presidents, a fishbowl into which those who disapprove of our very existence glare as they search for ammunition to use against us. Granted, every president, gay or straight, lives in a fishbowl. A presidency is a very public job; both on campus and in the community, the president is constantly watched and appraised. Every unmarried president has to be conscious of whose car is parked in the driveway at night. But LGBTQ presidents know that, single or married, there is no level of discretion, or banal domesticity, that will spare us accusations of impropriety or assertions that our lives damage our schools' reputations. LGBTQ presidents know that every unofficial guest in our homes is being scrutinized. Our relationships with our spouses are being evaluated. Too affectionate? Not affectionate enough? Who is "dominant"? Who greets visitors at the door? Who does the dishes? And there are no right answers. Any arrangement will be used against us.

None of this means, of course, that we should, or can afford to, ignore self-care. On the contrary, these extra stresses make such care all the more essential. At the same time, the responsibilities—to which we aspired and for which we offered ourselves—mean that we can't expect to limit our workdays to eight hours or our work weeks to five days. Nor can we, generally, expect to be able to enjoy all the vacation time our contracts allow for—even in the tamest of times. When crises arise, our plans may have to be jettisoned as we rise to the occasion. Routine, daily care that can be fitted into the often staccato rhythms of our lives, while we await the rarer opportunities for a spa day or a tropical getaway, are essential to a healthy presidency.

What might such care look like? I'd recommend starting with enough therapy to identify and begin to address your own triggers and blind spots: the things that annoy, worry, or terrify you. Beyond that, there are a multitude of ways to care for the body, mind, and spirit. Some take planning; some can be squeezed in between other obligations, on the way to meetings, or alongside the other daily tasks of life.

For what it's worth, here's what works for me:

- Meditation. The science shows that it calms the nervous system and helps the brain function better. Meditation also provides practice in deep breathing—making it as much a reflex as the pilot's instrument scan. Deep breathing settles the nervous system and keeps oxygen flowing to muscles and brain for optimal performance.
- Prayer. It reminds me who and Whose I am; who and how I aspire to be; and why I do the work I do. It reminds me that, no matter how much the pomp of office may tempt me to believe otherwise, I am not, in fact, the center of the universe—and I really don't want to be.
- Singing. I do it in the car (out of consideration for others). Singing, like meditation, regulates and deepens breathing. It relaxes me, awakens memories, and brings me joy.
- Kickboxing. Good for cardio and community. And hitting and kicking something *hard* is good not only for muscle

and bone but also, when frustrations have been piling up, for my spirit and state of mind.

- Whatever hobbies bring joy. For me: time with family, reading, flying, boating.
- Something to stretch the brain. Taking advantage of neuroplasticity to keep building brain reserves. For me, with degrees in the humanities, reading science and business journals presents new challenges. I'm considering learning a new language or taking up a new musical instrument, although I'm mindful that those may require more regular time in my schedule than is available now.

You already know about the value of good food and enough sleep. All the rest is a matter of what works for you.

The problematic paradox is that, even as the field of vision narrows just when we most need the fullest possible picture, so do both acute crises and chronic stress convince us that we have no time or energy for the very things that would better equip us to handle them. All the more reason to create a self-care regimen that works for you and to practice it until it becomes not just a habit but a reflex. Those we serve, those who follow our example, and those who aspire to follow in our footsteps deserve no less.

Theodora J. Kalikow

This is the context within which I consider self-care: our main job as administrators (president, dean, department chair) is to try to make good decisions about everything that comes our way. What we bring to this work is ourselves. Not a particular degree or academic field, but ourselves shaped by everything so far. (I think this is what people are trying to get at in searches when they ask for CVs and administrative philosophies: blunt instruments at best.) The point is, however, that our experience—the degrees, the life story, the adventures, the mistakes, the books read (or not read), the previous decisions . . . we bring all of it to every decision. In addition, as LGBTQ people we bring our particular history to this work. I have always considered this a valuable added expertise.

Perhaps a good analogy is to an opera singer. We don't have to sing, but just as their instrument is their mind and body, so is ours. They practice controlling operating conditions within themselves in order to get the musical results they want. We do the same to produce decision results. Therefore: if we want to bring the best instrument to our job, we need to take care of ourselves. Taking care means lot of the things your mother told you to do, but also a whole lot of things particular to you. Core: sleep, eat good food, stay hydrated, get some exercise, and take your vitamins. Stay away from bad chemicals. Other: do enough things that keep you in touch with yourself and your values and your family, whether it's a traditional, nontraditional, or one-of-a-kind family crafted just for you. I personally believe in novels and baseball, rowing and yoga. Also grandsons. And finally, processing time: you need some way to make sense of your experience so that you can access the lessons that life is teaching you. Some people do journaling.

Some people talk to trusted listeners. Others exercise and let their minds free-associate. Some meditate. As an introvert I know that I need time alone to get ready to return to the workplace, where

I deal with people all day and become, temporarily, an extrovert. Figure out what works for you.

The other thing is: If you are in a leadership position, your people need you to be relatively stable and predictable, the psychological "balance point" of the organization. You are leading here through example and consistency, which self-care can help you to maintain. If you haven't experienced this important but subtle leadership function, watch what happens in an organization when a key leader announces that their term is up soon. If you've ever turned over a rock and watched the ants scurry to move their eggs to safety, you'll see the institutional analogy.

Conversely, when you as a new leader arrive, one of your first jobs is to make the conditions such that everyone can relax, stop hiding the eggs, and get back to full organizational functionality. It doesn't happen overnight. This is aided by calm decisive sensible decision-making and just being a reasonable human being. (You don't have to be like your predecessor; you have to be like you, but consistency however you are is key.) They will be watching for your foibles, believe me, because they have to learn to navigate them. This is a time to especially practice self-care, restraint, and balance, even though you are all excited about starting a new job and want to run 24/7. Don't.

You need to take care of your team, not the other way around. Losing the balance point in an organization leads to danger and distorted ideas about power and influence. Your team will try to take care of you if they think you need it and you aren't doing it. Stifle this. Be in charge of you and train them not to micromanage, if possible. Or, graciously accept what your staff can help you with—it will make them feel wanted—but make sure it isn't serious personal self-care things (or other parts of your own job) that you should do yourself. In addition, your staff have to be invited to do their own self-care.

Whether it's family time, exercise time, special projects, or trips, your folks have to be convinced they can take that time in order to be an effective member of the team. Make sure they have what they need to be continuously effective. This means no expectations that they have to be available to you 24/7, and no routine panicked last-minute scrambles to accomplish a task. Once or twice a year—when the legislature or the board of trustees goes crazy or there is a real emergency—it's legitimate to call all hands on deck. But this shouldn't be a weekly occurrence.

If you find yourself living in a continuing state of crisis, you need to address this before you get very far in your administrative career. If you have a problem with getting things done on time, backwards-planning timetables and deadlines will save you. Education or business departments usually have several planning experts on board. If you happen to have a staff member who loves that stuff, put them in charge of organizational effectiveness and empower them to keep you all on task.

A final note: I have always thought that one essential item of self-care in our professional/personal portfolio is simply to be out. It protects us in numerous ways, and it normalizes the LGBTQ population in ways that are beneficial to everyone. In the olden days—the 1970s—I argued for being out because at that time, blackmail was a legitimate worry for LGBTQ people, or at least it was recognized as part of our story of the dangers of the hetero world and how to cope with them. For another thing, being out means you don't have to spend any mental energy pretending—about yourself, your family, about what you did on the weekend. Being out also means that you can be a positive role model for your LGBTQ students, faculty, staff, and even the wider public. For example, I always made sure to attend a meeting of the LGBTQ student group(s) for a special welcome at the beginning of the academic year, and I offer congratulations at the LGBTQ graduation celebration in the spring. Any president, provost, or dean could and should go too, of course, but our presence is extra special for our LGBTQ siblings. And celebrating the ones coming along is gratifying for us, too—a lovely occasion for both self-care and mentoring!

CHAPTER 10

Presidents and Partners

This chapter is about our experience, as well as others' perceptions, of perhaps our most important source of support, for those of us who are coupled. Because presidencies so often traditionally depend on the role of the couple, what are our experiences with a so-called nontraditional partner? Each of the authors of this chapter speaks to how their partnership with their spouse extends into their campus role. The first contributor, Ralph J. Hexter, the former president of a liberal arts college, writes about the role of his husband in the trajectory of his career and the ways in which their relationship had traditional and nontraditional implications for the campus. The next two contributors pen essays with their partners. James Gandre, the president of an urban music conservatory, writes with his husband, Boris Thomas, who is a psychotherapist and executive coach, about the integration of their relationship into the community of their school. Karen M. Whitney, the retired president of a rural public university, writes with her wife, Peggy L. Apple, a faculty member still teaching at the university's school of education, about making relationship decisions within a four-stage model that they propose to explain the life cycle of higher education presidencies.

Ralph J. Hexter

Anyone contemplating taking on the role of college or university president has to consider the impact on one's family. Whether the president lives in college-provided housing on campus or not, it is a 24/7 commitment that doesn't so much encroach on personal time and space as it erases the line between personal and private altogether.

After I had been a dean for several years, it dawned on me that a person in my position and with my credentials might well be considered presidential material. Was that something I was interested in? Maybe. The question was entirely theoretical because I assumed that my partner of many years would be uninterested in our embarking on such a venture.

Which requires me to get down to particulars.

Manfred and I met in 1979, standing in line to buy tickets for a gala New Year's evening performance at the Bavarian State Opera. The all-night line. In Munich's December cold. So, alignment check: two opera fanatics. But don't let the stereotypes run amok. Manfred is not an academic, which in German terms means that he didn't attend university. In the German tradition, his parents preferred that he "learn a trade," in his case precision mechanic, the basis for a long list of different jobs. The world of the university, much less that of American colleges and their peculiar cultural practices, was entirely foreign to him. He made many friends when he joined me in the United States soon after I became an untenured faculty member at Yale University, but he was made to feel monumentally uncomfortable at college functions.

To my surprise, two decades later, when first one and then another search team tried to lure me into the pool of presidential candidates, he warmed to the idea. And then, suddenly, it was showtime. A finalist interview with partners. Of course, he charmed one and all. He cleans up well, and I think many found his light but unmistakable German accent endearingly exotic. (As embarrassing and problematic as that may be, it's not something we could do anything about.)

The deal-closer may have been entirely his doing. After an exhausting first day on the Hampshire campus, I staggered into our room at the inn already pulling off my tie. "What are you doing?" he asked. "I'm exhausted." "I've been cooped up in this room all day. We're going out for a nightcap," he responded. Knowing better than to gainsay him, I put on my jacket again. Along the way, we happened to run into one of the students on the search committee, who was delighted to see us. And next morning, I learned that my boundless energy and epic indefatigability were already legendary. If they only knew!

So we moved to Amherst, Massachusetts. Part of our agreement was that if we made this shift, Manfred could retire. We were aware, of course, that by 2005, presidents and their other halves didn't all look the same—thank goodness—and that the "trailing spouse" didn't by any means need to fulfill the traditional role of "helpmeet." One of the memories Manfred retained from New Haven was that incoming Yale president Benno Schmidt's wife, Helen Whitney, famously said that she wasn't going "to pour tea."

Neither was Manfred. Male-male and female-female couples complicate traditional expectations of the roles each partner will play, offering a degree of freedom. Certainly, we felt free to depart from, or conform to, expectations of both president and presidential spouse. Rather conventionally, Manfred and I were co-hosts of all events at the house and social events on campus. He continued to be a favorite of trustees, anchoring tables at larger events, and I think alumni and parents of ultraliberal Hampshire College took genuine pleasure in "their" same-sex first couple. I like to think that all our students, however they identify, learned something by seeing a male-male couple in the second quarter-century of their relationship.

Perhaps the most unconventional feature of our couplehood, as I noted above, was that we are "mismatched" in terms of education. I could write reams on the pretensions of so many in our university world, but all of it simply puzzled Manfred, who never pretended his background was other than it was. Over the years he had held many jobs, from insurance salesman to general contractor to realtor to creator of prototypes in the early days of additive manufacturing. To come to Hampshire, he retired from driving a school bus, but we smiled that in the minds of some trustees this was translated into his having "sold his bus company."

An interesting analog to this is that Manfred had an easy accord with all the people who really make the college run, whether the groundskeepers or the maintenance team. The unusual dividend for me was that this college president heard of concerns across the campus very early on and from the widest possible circles. Perhaps the most important weekly meeting at the college was the "kitchen cabinet" that Manfred convened in the president's residence on Fridays with the house manager and my chief-of-staff.

Since we were in Massachusetts, the opportunity to marry came early, and we did so on September 1, 2007. (We may in fact be the first legally wed same-sex college presidential couple in the United States, but perhaps we will discover otherwise.) Not long after our marriage, the smallest and most intimate affair in the president's residence you could possibly imagine, we hosted a celebration on campus to which all community members were invited. As we approached, I could see that some chalking was being washed off the pavement. After inquiring, I was told that members of the queer community had protested the "heteronormativity" of our marriage. A classic "only Hampshire" moment, to be sure, but I wish I could have had a discussion with the students, for I can certainly sympathize with some of what I imagine their arguments were.

Manfred was quick to adopt the title of "husband." When Hampshire was undergoing review by our regional accrediting association, at dinner a member of the visiting committee asked Manfred what his role was. "I'm the president's husband," he replied. You could see the wheels slowly turning in the man's head until the penny dropped. Fortunately, in Massachusetts at least, many soon grew accustomed to men who had a husband. While on a fundraising trip out west, I learned that Manfred had been hospitalized. As I flew back, I called the hospital, and upon identifying myself as the patient's husband was immediately given all essential information, welcome comfort at a time of anxiety and a sign of the respect and consideration that all families everywhere should receive without question.

For all the pleasant aspects of the experience, we were both happy when I left the presidency and assumed the role of university provost at University of California, Davis. Once again we could live in a home of our own, and Manfred didn't need anyone's permission to move a shelf or a picture.

There is a coda to this story, a temporary reprise of first couplehood, which occurred when I become the university's acting chancellor within the space of three hours. During this interim assignment, we didn't have to live in the chancellor's residence, though we hosted events there. Still, UC Davis's Intercollegiate Athletics Division 1 status afforded Manfred a range of other new experiences. Though he doesn't much care for American football, he did take to holding forth in the chancellor's box at football games as well as rooting for both the men's and women's basketball teams. Indeed, might we in 2017 have been the first same-sex "first couple" hosted by the National Collegiate Athletic Association for March Madness?

James Gandre and Boris Thomas

As Boris rounds the corner at West 122nd Street and Broadway, the southeast corner of Manhattan School of Music's vertical campus, and starts walking the short city block to Claremont Avenue, where the school's main entrance is located, he waves to a student and then a faculty member who are headed out. Making a right onto Claremont Avenue, he approaches the head of security, who is standing outside the school's oldest and main building, taking a break and stretching her legs. She grew up in the neighborhood and has been a devoted employee for 20 years. They greet each other with a hug, and she asks him if he had a good workout. Boris has come from the gym at Columbia University, a facility shared by the seven higher education institutions situated in a ten-block long area that encompasses most of our Morningside Heights neighborhood. They talk a bit about her workout boot camp, for which she wakes up at 4 a.m. He wishes her a great day and proceeds past the main entrance, stopping for a moment to greet a faculty member and congratulate her on her concert the week before; then he heads toward the second building on the campus, Andersen Hall, which houses the residence hall, most administrative offices, performance halls and, on top, at the eighteenth floor, an apartment that serves as the president's residence. The security lead for this building looks tired. Boris queries her, and she tells him that she was up all night assembling party favors for her daughter's sweet sixteen. They chat about the theme of the party, and Boris reminds her that she needs her rest. Boris steps into the elevator with a student who is traveling from the basement laundry facilities up to his dorm room. He is carrying two huge laundry bags, and Boris kids him about how long he let the washing pile up. The student laughs and gets off on the fifteenth floor. At the eighteenth floor Boris enters the home we share, a very important part of the life of this small institution. In the president's residence, from September to June, we host numerous post- and preperformance receptions, board of trustee and donor dinners, faculty appreciation ceremonies, a variety of alumni events, and mini-concerts. In August, there's an ice cream social for incoming and returning students. In winter, we host dinners for student affinity groups, and in December and June, respectively, there are a staff and faculty holiday party and a terrace barbecue.

People come to the apartment and are never shooed out. The talk is that everyone feels welcome in the residence and that we enjoy their visits.

In many ways similar to some aspects of the president's role, we've described elements of the first spouse's day on a small campus, whether it's interactions with security, the faculty, the students, or the board of trustees.

Most presidential couples, unlike any others on campus, whether straight or LGBTQ, are likely seen as inseparable units, intricate parts of the fabric of the institutions they serve; indeed, in their roles as president and first spouse, they are often the center of the entire enterprise. Performing this role may be easy for many, as it is most often for us, but it does not come without stress due to at times feeling a need to be less measured and more authentic when things are not quite right. But that kind of authenticity is not practical or advised. Jim recalls comments by the renowned president of the University of Maryland, Baltimore County, Freeman A. Hrabowski III, during an institute for new presidents that he attended during the first year of his presidency. Hrabowski said: "Presidents are the embodiment of the institution. When you are energetic and happy, the institution is energetic and happy. When you are tired or sick, the institution is tired or sick. When you are visibly annoyed, the institution must have problems. Thus, you must always appear to be vibrant, engaged, warm, friendly, and ultimately positive even when you are not." As an extension of that concept, the first couple must always look energetic, engaged, warm, friendly with others and with each other, and ultimately positive.

As an LGBTQ couple, we feel that the symbolism of the first couple takes on a different and special meaning for many within the campus community. Jim welcomes students and their parents at curbside when they drive up on move-in day and helps them unpack their cars. Later that day, at the welcome convocation for students and their families, he tells them that since he *and his husband* also live in the residence hall, as their neighbors we will look forward to seeing them in the building as our paths cross in the common areas. In that convocation he makes it explicit, in the most matter-of-fact and normalized way, that we are a same-gender couple.

As people outside the dominant (heterosexual) group, LGBTQ couples like us are often the objects of more attention, extra-watchful eyes, and perhaps even higher levels of scrutiny. On the other hand, for some students who see themselves as "other," as an out, multiracial couple, we are sometimes seen as anchors for them, our presence giving them a sense of security, belonging, and personal potential. We try to stay cognizant of this fact and not to underestimate the power of our presence to the campus community, particularly for the students, who come from a myriad of cultures, religions, and types of family units in more than fifty countries and nearly fifty states. An example of this impact was brought home at one of our gatherings in the residence for our campus LGBTQ group when we asked the group how they felt when they first heard that Jim was gay and that he had a husband. A Taiwanese student, who offered how difficult it was for him to even contemplate being out in his country and with his parents, simply replied, "I felt I would be safe."

Being the president and first spouse on any campus is a gift, a tremendous privilege, honor, and responsibility. It offers the couple the broadest set of potential relationships and interactions of any on a campus. At times, being the first couple also comes with a fair amount of stress, stress that comes from the packed schedule we normally keep and the constant, personal examination not experienced by any other couple on campus. But, being an LGBTQ first couple opens the possibilities for service to on the community that we believe has the potential to be felt in ways that are significantly different from that of a traditional, heterosexual couple. As an LGBTQ couple, we can help reshape students' perceptions of what is normal and good. By our presence and example, we can help those who are closeted to move toward self-acceptance, building pride in themselves, and ultimately live an authentic life that is theirs and not governed by others' beliefs about who they should be.

We've come down from the president's residence, headed out for dinner. Stopping at the security desk, Boris gets his usual ribbing from the evening security guard, who tells Boris he is "too difficult and needs to be good." They laugh, as always. It's their schtick. We walk to our local Italian restaurant a block away, in many ways an extension of the school, where we are greeted with hugs by the jocular owner. He tells us that we just missed two of the school's faculty members.

Everyone is connected.

We feel at home.

Indeed, this is one of the best versions of family, and we're proud to be part of it.

Karen M. Whitney and Peggy L. Apple

College presidents and their presidencies are often studied in order to understand their successes or failures. What is less often considered is that a spouse, partner, or other member of the president's family is also part of "the presidency." The presidency is more than the person holding the title. It is in fact the community of internal and external stakeholders who support, connect, oversee, and are impacted by the president. The intentional or unintentional attitudes and actions of a spouse actually contribute to the success or failure of a presidency. Given the often extraordinary attention that comes with being a LGBTQ presidential couple, the risks can be greater; often it's the president's family that is most affected by the presidency. As we observed earlier, "the spouse has a unique connection to the president unlike any other person. This connection undoubtedly influences, how university personnel engage the spouse"(Apple and Whitney 2009, 60). Even more so, when presidents are LGBTQ, they are most vividly LGBTQ to their constituencies when they are at events or in public with their spouse.

To successfully navigate the challenges of serving as a LGBTQ college presidential couple, it is important to recognize and reflect on the similar experiences that all presidential couples encounter, as well as the unique experiences specific to LGBTQ couples. We believe that the "presidential life cycle" comprises four stages: aspiring, acquiring, attending, and adjourning.

The aspire stage is the time to talk about "fit" and the role your spouse would hope to have (or not have) as a presidential spouse. With more than 4,300 institutions of higher learning in the United States (Chronicle of Higher Education 2020), there are 4,300 variations of "fit" or "misfit." Each institution has its own history, culture, mission, vision, and values that will shape what is expected from both the president and the spouse. The key at this stage is to come to an understanding of what aspects of "fit" are important to both of you and to use this as a "fit-filter" in deciding which opportunities to pursue. In some presidencies, the role of the spouse is no different from that of spouses of other university leaders. At other institutions, the spouse may hold a substantial role in the life of the campus. During this stage, we considered how a presidency might impact our life as a couple. Since both of our careers are in higher education, we had the opportunity to observe many presidencies, and we began to develop an ideal image of what "our presidency" might look like. We talked about what we would enjoy and not enjoy since we both believe that being a president is a 24/7 experience. These exchanges were helpful as we moved to the next stage.

The acquiring stage involves evaluating presidential opportunities and entering the search and hiring process. Reviewing the institution's policies regarding spouses is particularly important for LGBTQ couples, who inevitably are challenging traditional gender roles. During the acquiring stage, as you and your spouse identify institutions that might be of interest and you begin to submit your applications, you need to research each campus that you're considering. What will life be like for my spouse in this community? As you study the campus's history and culture, investigate the past and current roles of the president's spouse. To what extent does the spouse define their own role? Does the spouse attend, host, or play a prominent role in campus and community events? It's important to study policies for guidance. For instance, a policy could make clear whether the spouse can be employed by the university. A policy should indicate any expectations for the spouse and the parameters of any compensation. (Typically the presidential spouse serves as an unpaid volunteer.) As you and your spouse explore and talk through these points, the characteristics of the ideal appointment will emerge. Clarion University had no formal policy on spouses, and we had to rely on insights from the search professional and short discussions with key stakeholders during the search process. Fortunately, our expectations of what Peggy's role would be turned out to align with the history and customary role of the spouse at Clarion, but the alignment was a happy accident.

The most successful LGBTQ presidential couples are comfortable with who they are. In being upfront about your LGBTQ identity, what are the other aspects of fit that you need to add to your filter? Does an urban or rural setting make a difference to you? In small towns, people will know when you are at the grocery or will pull up a chair to join you for breakfast at the local diner. If the campus has a presidential residence, your family will be engaged in social events in your "home," and the housekeeper from facilities will know more about your personal life than if your home is off campus. Is this good for you and your spouse? As an LGBTQ couple, additional aspects of fit may include challenges to traditional gender roles or at least some initial role confusion by stakeholders. For instance, what is the culture regarding LGBTQ citizens in the local community? Does the campus have institutionalized supports for LGBTQ students and employees?

The attending stage is the longest stage of the presidency, lasting from the issuance of the public announcement that the new president has been hired to the moment, hopefully many years later, that the president is leaving. Just as in the aspiring and acquiring stages, open communication and clear expectations of the spousal role is vital. We both worked to cultivate solid relationships with key stakeholders, particularly the board chair, the head of the Pennsylvania state university system, and the executive team.

As an LGBTQ couple, we took a keen interest in studying the university's history and culture and the communities that Clarion serves. The key to our success was that we were very clear about Peggy's role, first with each other and then in our communications with stakeholders. At the beginning of the presidency, we had to educate others on how to refer to us. Many wanted to refer to Peggy as my "friend"; I quickly made it known that she was my "partner." Once we married, we referred to each other as spouses.

Adjourning a presidency is often overlooked in the literature and warrants discussion. This final stage in the presidential life cycle is about completing the appointment and securing one's legacy, and it includes celebrating the president's spouse and family. As the president works with key stakeholders in crafting an "exit plan" or off-boarding process, it is important that the spouse be properly recognized and that their role have closure. We made it clear in announcements and celebrations that occurred during the last months of the presidency that we were each being recognized and celebrated.

As more LGBTQ leaders become college presidents and bring their families to these presidencies, understanding the stages of a presidency is important. Understanding and proactively planning and preparing for the additional challenges as a LGBTQ presidential couple is priceless. A presidency is a wonderful and special way to contribute to higher education, and it's a journey made better if you can share it together.

REFERENCES

Apple, P., and K. Whitney. 2019. The Presidential Spouse Role: How a Thoughtful Policy Can Guide the Way. *Change: The Magazine for Higher Education* 51 (1): 58–61.

Chronicle of Higher Education. 2020. *The Almanac of Higher Education, 2019–20.* Washington, DC: Chronicle of Higher Education. https://www.chronicle.com/specialreport/The-Almanac-of-Higher/267.

CHAPTER 11

Becoming an LGBTQ President or Leader

This chapter is direct advice framed by our experience as LGBTQ leaders in higher education. The contributors are Karen M. Whitney, a retired chancellor of a rural public university who has continued in interim chancellor roles; James Gandre, the president of an urban music conservatory; and Katherine Hancock Ragsdale, a former president of a divinity school who now serves as president of an international advocacy and membership organization. Each author addresses the upsides and downsides of the presidency and offers advice for LGBTQ people about the search and selection process, as well as about strategies for making the job work. Their essays describe paths to the presidency, but their counsel applies equally to getting and succeeding in other leadership roles in higher education.

Karen M. Whitney

While there are many paths to becoming and succeeding as a college president, I believe that every president generally experiences the same presidential life-cycle, which is composed of four stages: aspiring, acquiring, attending, and adjourning. I have come to this perspective based upon my own experience as a college president. I had the privilege of serving as the sixteenth president of Clarion University for seven years and then concluded my appointment as the interim chancellor for the Pennsylvania State System of

Higher Education for one year. To reflect on the presidential experience, I have translated my experiences into a leadership model with the hope that you will evaluate and create your own plan of action.

I didn't seriously aspire to or specifically prepare for a presidency until about a year before I actually submitted my credentials for a position. So you could say that my "aspiring stage" was rather brief. I did spend many years preparing to be a vice president, during which I considered leadership developing experiences and honed key areas of expertise. I served as a vice chancellor and executive officer of a large complex university for eleven years, which was valuable preparation. Whenever you begin your serious interest in a presidency, I suggest that you consider the leadership or management experiences and areas of expertise that you might want to cultivate over time. This is also the time (as mentioned in chapter 8), to include your significant other in this exploration. It's important to engage the important people in your life at this stage if you aspire to having both a successful relationship and a future presidency. The aspire stage is the time to think about what a great fit would look like for you and those close to you. For me, fit was the extent to which the institution's location, mission, vision, values, priorities, power base, history, and culture were in alignment with who I am and how I lead.

About a year before I applied for a presidential position, I reflected deeply about what matters most to me as a higher education leader and presidential wannabe. I created my "fit-filter," which I used to sift through what mattered most to me. In my fit-filter I included my vision, mission, and goals for my leadership. I also included a list of preferred institutional characteristics and a list of who I thought I could work with and who could work with me. I began to gain a clarity about myself and the institution that I might lead. I knew that I could be a great president, but the question for me was which university would value my leadership? As an out lesbian, my task was to locate a university that had a power base, culture, and history that would be in accord with my values and would be willing to take a risk in hiring me.

The items in my filter included the type of institution: public or private; religious or secular; the location: rural or urban, west coast or east coast; research or teaching-intensive; two-year or four-year; part of a system or stand-alone; well funded or "a turnaround." The students mattered, and so I considered what it was about the students that would inspire my leadership. There were certain types of students that "spoke to me" and might speak to you: first-generation; of a certain socioeconomic status; majority women, historically black, or Hispanic-serving might influence your fit. I also looked at the LGBTQ climate in the institution, community, and state. I looked at the historical roles of the presidential family or spouse, and I wanted to consider what might be expected from my spouse and family. Based on my fit-filter, my strengths, and my past accomplishments, I choose which positions to consider.

My next stage was to "acquire" a position. This was the stage of evaluating specific presidential opportunities and entering the search process. Using my fit-filter, I reached out to head hunters I'd met over the years to consider which searches to enter. I looked for positions where I felt I met all the minimum qualification (and most of the preferred qualifications) and where I saw an alignment with how I wished to lead and manage. I examined the history, culture, and politics of the community and institution. I reviewed the institution's strategic plan, news articles, accreditation reports, mention of lawsuits, minutes of faculty senate and board meetings, and everything I could find online. I read about the current president, their public statements, writings, and talks. I looked at all the institutional policies and particularly ones that related to executives. I tried to locate any policy that might relate to the presidential spouse or family. I was a detective discovering the inner workings of the institution. In the end, on July 1, 2010, I was hired to serve as Clarion University's sixteenth president.

Now that I had the job I was determined to keep it. I call this stage the "attending stage." This stage begins the moment a public announcement is issued that you have been hired to the moment, hopefully many years later, that you announce that you will be stepping down. During this stage I focused on my brand or "presidential reputation." I thought a great deal about how I showed up to my presidency. My brand was represented in my everyday actions. As president, everyone really does watch you and judge you. How you choose to present yourself is significant to a successful presidency. My showing up also included being a very out lesbian with a spouse of 25 years. It was crucially important that I was very comfortable with myself—so comfortable, in fact, that I was able to help others be comfortable with me and my spouse. This comfort space was key to building and maintaining relationships as a president. Equally important is understanding how my identity related to the history and culture of the institution. While I was the first out lesbian, I was not the first women president. I was fine not having multiple firsts to navigate. To keep fresh and forward looking, every summer of my presidency I took stock of what I had accomplished and reflected on the time and context in which I was leading. I sought critical feedback from many in order to learn, reflect, and adjust my leadership and management for the next year.

Adjourning a presidency is the last stage and most often overlooked in the literature. I have to admit that this was the stage that I paid the least attention to and I regret not being more thoughtful about what I and my spouse needed as we concluded this appointment. For me, this stage is about how to end and transition out graciously. It's about completing the appointment and securing one's legacy.

This stage began the moment I thought about leaving. To mitigate the downside, prior to the public announcement I developed an exit plan and out-boarding process in close collaboration with the board chair. Looking back, I should have done more planning and perhaps gotten feedback from current and former presidents. I made sure that I included my spouse in the exit plan since in many respects it was her presence in the presidency that made our LGBTQ identity most vivid, and I was determined that she be appropriately recognized as a loyal and engaged presidential spouse.

The public announcement of my exiting was both a relief and an overwhelming experience. Once the announcement occurred, I went into a completely different leadership space. In an instant, everyone associated with my presidency treated me differently. It was neither good nor bad; it was just different. A few folks who often enjoyed fighting with me (think rage against the machine), simply evaporated once they knew I was leaving. I knew that once one announces an exit, the institution instantly pivots to securing and on-boarding the next president. it's an odd and lonely feeling. I focused on my road ahead and let the institution move on.

While no one leader can be all things to all people, there are smart ways to look at a presidency and to consider how you can organize yourself to succeed. Considering "Whitney's Stages of a College Presidency" coupled with the importance of developing your own fit-filter is a way to manage your path to the presidency and ensure your success.

James Gandre

It has been my great privilege to work in higher education as a proud member of the LGBTQ+ community for nearly 40 years, and I cannot conceive of any other work that would be more fulfilling. I came to college from a working-class family in Sheboygan, Wisconsin. By the time I entered college, my exposure to life beyond my home state was limited to five short trips: to Chicago, Houston, Indianapolis, Washington, DC, and Toronto. College opened doors for me and exposed me to vistas that I never knew existed. My world expanded exponentially during each of my four years in college and ultimately transformed my life. Part of that transformation was my own coming out in 1979 during my junior year.

What drove me to be a leader in higher education has a simple answer. Since my own life was transformed by education, I wanted to dedicate it to transforming students' lives and in the process to making society just a bit better. For me, nothing is more sacred than the bond of trust that each student places in the institution to deliver on this promise of real change. From my first job as an admissions counselor to director of career planning, from chief enrollment officer to a college dean, and then to provost and finally college president, each job has fulfilled my personal mission of transformation and has as a consequence brought me great joy and a remarkable sense of fulfillment.

The first question I always ask people who come to me for counsel about being a president is "Why do you want to be a president?" You need to consider this simple question because, while such jobs are often extraordinarily rewarding, enjoyable, and gratifying, they also impose a heavy burden. The president carries significant responsibility and, for smaller institutions like mine, nearly ultimate authority for the institution's future. A president must be available 24/7 and he/she/they is on display and watched much of each day, including evenings and weekends as well as, for those who live on campus, at home. Like female leaders, leaders of color, or leaders of any other underrepresented group, LGBTQ leaders face a concomitant burden of being judged and watched more closely than, say, a straight white male. This extra challenge often requires us to work harder, better, faster, and longer.

I talk about these issues with would-be presidents not to complain but to make sure they are aware of what to expect. If the mission to transform lives and to be a servant leader is not clear and strong enough, then the burdens of the presidency may overwhelm the individual's spirit, damaging for both the individual or institution they serve. I have watched too many colleagues pursue a presidency because they were "qualified," because someone told them "you could be a president," or because they had climbed the proverbial ranks and this seemed the obvious next step. Many don't achieve that sought-after presidency because being qualified to be a president is only one basic ingredient in seeking one. Others assumed presidencies only to lose them because they had not pursued the job for reasons that spoke to their core values and abilities.

Once you are able to answer honestly why you want to be a leader, understand the associated challenges, and believe you can be a successful president, you need to consider how to search for the right presidency. If you know yourself well, the searches you enter will be accordingly limited to institutions that fit you. Here, too, I have seen far too many colleagues pursue jobs that were not a good fit for them or for the institution, and if they were appointed, those presidencies most often did not go well. For those of us in the LGBTQ+ community, being clear about how you fit in a particular college or university community is perhaps even more essential than it is for our heterosexual counterparts. I limited my searches for a presidency based on geographic locations and type of institution, mission, and campus environment, among other things. Even with my research and careful planning, I found myself in the wrong place several times. In three out of the five searches for which I was a finalist, a member of the search committees told me that I was the leading candidate but that I was not chosen because trustees were not comfortable with the idea of a gay president. In the long run, I was thankful I was not chosen for those jobs.

The other part of success in a search for a presidency is being able to easily answer this essential question: Why is it important that I become the president of this institution at this moment in time? If you cannot answer that question easily, your presidency will not be as successful as one for which you have a clear and unequivocal answer.

If you get through the search gauntlet and are appointed president, there is the role of actually *being* the president. At my installation ceremony, Chuck Middleton, then president of Roosevelt University, an institution that I served for thirteen years before coming to Manhattan School of Music, said, "The modern college president must have the wisdom of Solomon, the patience of Job, and the stomach of a goat." All assembled chuckled, but few knew how sage and prescient those words were. Wisdom, patience, and a cast-iron stomach, although not all one needs, are essential components of a successful presidency. I understood what he meant intellectually, but I didn't fully understand or feel what he was saying that day since I was still in my "honeymoon" period. My experiences during the past seven years have shown me that truer words were never spoken. Although my life as a president has been overwhelmingly positive and rewarding, it has come with burdens I had never experienced before and challenges that I never expected and hope never to relive (including a pandemic!), not because they were unsolvable, but because they were tough situations, called for real fortitude, and distracted from the positive work of moving the institution forward.

I conclude this essay where I began: I have been truly privileged to work in higher education and cannot imagine a better vocation for myself. My presidency has been magical, wonderful, and immensely rewarding. I believe that I found an ideal fit with my institution and it with me, and much of that was due to the institution embracing me as an openly gay man. Together, my community has achieved so much, and our students and faculty have been well served. But the presidency has also come with unexpected challenges that ultimately rest on my shoulders alone.

Consequently, knowing yourself—knowing what motivates you, what gives you energy and satisfaction, and what you find intolerable—will lead you to deciding whether an institution is right for you and you are right for the institution you will serve. If all of this aligns well, I hope that you'll be as glad as I am that you pursued this wonderful journey.

Katherine Hancock Ragsdale

The academic presidency has been described, rightly in my opinion, as one of the most challenging and frustrating, as well as one of the most fulfilling and rewarding, vocations imaginable. When the fit between the nature of the work in general, the culture and needs of the particular institution, and the temperament and skills of the individual president is apt, the outcome can be joyous. Discerning the right fit with a particular institution is vital, but long before that step, it is important to discern whether a presidency of any sort is the right match for your nature and your dreams.

Presidencies take many shapes, and there are many paths that can lead to them. I am not a career academic, and the school of which I was president was a small professional graduate school—a divinity school. I did not come to the presidency through the institutional ranks but as an alumna of the school, called back to the presidency on the basis of my success in the profession and as a leader of many nonprofits. I have observed the path to tenure and up through the academic ranks, and I have facilitated it for others, but it is not the path that I walked.

Such alternative paths are less the exception than they once were. The Association of Governing Boards, the *Chronicle of Higher Education*, and various other reliable sources suggest that a steadily increasing number of presidents are coming from nontraditional paths, from outside the academic system. This doesn't surprise me. Leading an established institution doesn't require the ability to do any of the other jobs in or of the institution; that's what the rest of the staff are for. What *is* required is the ability to lead a complex institution (which includes the ability to *refrain* from doing other people's jobs). So let's talk not about traditional pathways to academic leadership but about the skills and temperament necessary to lead.

First, a question: Why choose to be a leader, a president, in the first place? The stresses are enormous. In every other position, there is someone, somewhere, to whom you can hand off important but intractable problems. Not so for the president. Crises never stop, and they always seem to land on the president's desk. Every issue that leaves staff feeling overwhelmed eventually falls into the president's lap. The temptation to feel that you alone carry the ultimate responsibility for the life of the institution and the fulfillment of its mission is constant and ubiquitous.

As if these burdens weren't more than enough, I've noticed that women are often not afforded the opportunity to lead unless and until an institution is in serious trouble. We're called in when there's a mess to be cleaned up—when the challenges of leadership are more pronounced and the opportunities to reap its rewards will be, at best, deferred. I suspect that this may be true of other marginalized candidates, as well. And on top of that, our own communities within the institution often expect us to be their saviors, dismantling, by our very presence, the systems that have marginalized and oppressed them. At the same time, these communities frequently have an understandable distrust of power. So, when we exercise the power of our office to fulfill our responsibilities, to turn around troubled institutions, and to create justice within those institutions, our own communities may turn on us, accusing us of having abandoned our marginalized status in order to identify with oppressive power structures.

Why would anyone choose such a job? A good question and one that we who are used to defying the odds and accomplishing the impossible ought to consider carefully. Is the troubled institution to which we may be called capable of being saved? Is it willing to make the changes necessary to overcome the challenges that threaten it? Are there reliable allies available? Are we prepared for rejection not only by homophobes but perhaps even by those within our own communities who are suspicious of all authority?

If the answer to these and similar questions is yes, it just might be that you are not only capable of a successful presidency but that it might be a source not only of satisfaction but also of great joy. Again, why opt for this job?

Apart from the fulfillment, and fun, of addressing big challenges, there's the joy of making a difference. In *How Will You Measure Your Life?*, Clay Christensen of Harvard Business School reflected on a company picnic as a moment when the joy of management became clear to him. He watched staff with their families and realized that, as a manager, he was positioned to be either a positive or negative influence in all of their lives. His management would help determine whether employees left work feeling competent, challenged, appreciated, and creative or frustrated, demeaned, underutilized, and bored. And he had the power to help determine which one of those people walked through the door at home that night. Which person did children and partners spend their evenings and weekends with? The presidency offers myriad opportunities to make a difference—in the lives of our students and our staffs, in the life and mission of our institutions, in the communities of which the school and its varied constituents are a part.

So, if you find an unceasing array of challenges more invigorating than daunting, if the opportunity to make a difference in more lives and in more ways than you'll ever be able to know brings you joy, if you crave a life of demanding service, then perhaps a presidency is what you're looking for.

What, then, are the skills and temperament required to lead complex institutions? Here are a few:

- A willingness, and ability, to see all the many, many balls in the air *and yet* to step away from the instinct to take over the juggling. This is hard. It's our extreme (or at least above average) competence (and for many LGBTQ people, women, people of color, etc., my money is on "extreme") that allowed us to advance to a point where a presidency seems within reach. We got here by solving problems; doing everything in front of us, and then some, very, very well. We're used to being superheroes flying to the rescue. It's in our nature and, as members of marginalized, under-represented communities, it has been a survival skill. But as presidents we need, instead, to . . .

- Delegate and empower. I don't care how amazing you are; you cannot handle every crisis, or even every routine function, of a complex institution. You need good staff who know that they have your confidence. And you can neither develop nor maintain such a staff if you exhibit a lack of confidence by swooping in to micromanage.
- Coach. A strong leader must not only avoid sapping others' confidence by over-functioning but must actively, as a primary presidential responsibility, nurture their confidence and coach them to their own successes, building their competence and their authority.
- Stay calm so that others can. Panic doesn't help. Those who run around with their hair on fire just start more fires. The president should be a non-anxious presence who creates a climate of low anxiety and high confidence.
- Accept the blame and share the glory.

If you enjoy having all your ducks in a row, organizing a project and seeing it through to the finish, and seeing concrete results, then there are many jobs in which you can excel and feel fulfilled, knowing that you're an important contributor and an asset to the institution; a presidency, however, is probably not one of those jobs. Yes, there is the occasional clear success, the reaching of a goal. But no sooner will you get that new department or program designed, approved, and staffed than the implementation problems will start pouring in. Even as you and your development department celebrate finalizing a major gift, some new crisis will be brewing: fire, mold, star faculty denied a visa, active shooter, #MeToo charge, frat hazing death, a global pandemic . . .

But if you delight in the opportunity to make a real difference in many lives; if you enjoy nonstop challenges, can manage your stress, can build a team that you can count on, and, with their help, resist the urge to do it all yourself, you may be ready for a presidency—and the immediate challenge of finding the right presidency for you.

CHAPTER 12

The Future of the LGBTQ Presidency and Leadership

This book was conceived in the middle of the Trump administration, but prior to the COVID-19 pandemic and the renewed activism that followed the murders of George Floyd and Breonna Taylor. Across our conversations, the contributors to this volume wondered together about what this particular and strange time means for higher education and LGBTQ rights. Do LGBTQ presidents bring something unique to present crises, such as questioning assumptions about who can or should lead and what might be emerging roles for higher education in protecting human rights? What will happen when or if more large, prestigious, rural, or southern universities hire LGBTQ presidents? Is progress inevitable, or are we in a fragile moment for higher education and LGBTQ and other human rights? We asked one of our group, Ralph J. Hexter—the former president of a private liberal arts college and former interim chancellor of a large public research university, who at the time had returned to teaching after serving as provost of a large California public university for nearly a decade—to speak to these questions.

For the final essay in this volume, I've been asked to look to the future. Obviously, lacking prophetic powers, I will venture no predictions. Rather, I will focus on what I think ought to happen—or at least what I very much want to happen. I begin, as the future must, with the foundation of the past and present.

Not long before I sat down to write these words, we celebrated the fiftieth anniversary of the Stonewall Riots. We now have a much fuller picture both of the activism that predated Stonewall—for example, the Compton's Cafeteria Riots in San Francisco in 1966—and the true diversity of those who did most of the resisting on that New York night in June 1969 that has ever since been regarded as a turning-point in the gay movement. In no small way it was. The fact that the Stonewall Inn was, to use a term not yet current in 1969, a gender-queer space was long obscured, even ignored; gay popular history celebrated it as the birth of "gay" pride. And while it was by no means a white space, people of color were bleached out of the story in a process all too familiar in the (white) American imaginary. In similar fashion, the mainline narrative failed to do justice to the critically important involvement of women from the earliest days, although that injustice, too, is gradually being repaired. (My brief epilogue can only touch on the multiple paths of queer history, including gay and lesbian histories, but also extending far beyond.)

The face of the emerging gay subculture that the public saw, given the asymmetries that existed then and to a large extent still do, was disproportionately white, male, and urban. It is disappointing but in no way surprising, considering the long history of power relations, that while the increasingly vocal subculture gained new degrees of freedom the gains were greatest for those traditionally most privileged in American society.

It is of course impossible to generalize about the experiences of many: even before the idea of a gay identity was in wide circulation, many children and adolescents felt alienated from expectations and norms in a way they themselves could not easily name. Still, a significant number of those who came out in the first decade after Stonewall had been conditioned as children to be fully privileged as heterosexual as well as white and male and thus brought to the burgeoning movement, for better and for worse, the habits and expectation of empowerment.

This was to the good when it came to the relatively rapid process of entering the political sphere. In terms of men, and indeed women, who ran for office and got elected—all white—one recalls Elaine Noble, elected to the Massachusetts State Legislature in 1975; Harvey Milk, elected to the San Francisco Board of Supervisors in 1977 and tragically assassinated in 1978; and Barney Frank, also from Massachusetts, elected to the US House of Representatives in 1981. It was also a powerful force later in the 1980s after the emergence of AIDS: the speed with which organizations were launched to assist individuals and to demand that the medical establishment respond to the epidemic empowered a significant portion of those who were experiencing this devastating health crisis at first hand, even if ACT UP (the AIDS Coalition to Unleash Power) modeled a more radical and more inclusive style of activism (see now Schulman 2021). Nonetheless, the organization's effectiveness—in fundraising and in gaining public awareness and certain powerful allies—owed a great deal to the connections, financial resources, and political clout that its members had or could muster to advance their cause.

I do not for one second mean to imply that it was easy, nor do I want to replicate in this account the very erasure that I critiqued above of the significant contributions of men of color, women, and the emerging transsexual community. I want merely to establish that it shouldn't surprise us that when a new group emerges on the scene and begins to enter into positions of power, the asymmetries of power in society at large are often—one is tempted to say inevitably—replicated in the distribution of power and authority, even among the minoritized subset.

So it is that when the first set of "openly gay" college and university presidents were identified—the phrase comes from a series of articles in the *Chronicle of Higher Education* that ran between 2007 and 2011—the presidents were, with a few significant exceptions, predominantly white and male. The primary variation on the standard power asymmetries involved gender, although exactly how remains to be fully unpacked; it is one chapter in the richly complex interlacement of gay and lesbian histories that I referenced above. As a group, the first lesbian college presidents found themselves at the intersection of two circles, both of which were rarely represented in higher education's top leadership positions: women college presidents and gay college presidents. The complex interaction of the two phenomena deserves careful and multidimensional study.

Undeniable, however, is the fact that the majority of the first generation of self-identifying gay and lesbian presidents were white, no different in that regard from the overwhelming majority of all US college and university presidents. And since many of the first set were at private, generally urban and nondenominational institutions, some of the sectors within higher education in which one might expect more racial and ethnic diversity—the public universities, community (i.e., two-year) colleges, historically black colleges and universities—were grossly underrepresented.

Soon after 2010, this began to change, and the diversification of both gay and lesbian presidents and the types of institutions appointing them began. There has not been as much progress as I for one would like to have seen, but it is with this historical context as our foundation that I set forth the first and I believe most important desideratum for the future: even as gay and lesbian presidents bring visibility to one dimension of diversity, they themselves must become more diverse along other dimensions. To use memberships in LGBTQ Presidents in Higher Education as a census, roughly a hundred college or university presidents publicly identify as

LGBTQ to this point. By 2030, I would like to see that number surpass 250, ideally by a good bit. Even more importantly, I would like these presidents to be diverse along other vectors as well, starting with ethnicity (e.g., African American, Latinx, Asian/Pacific Islander, and Native American), but also including, for example, people with disabilities. I mean these as a partial listing of categories. Indeed, even within the membership of LGBTQ Presidents in Higher Education, no doubt an imperfect proxy but perhaps the best we have, we are aware of only a few who identify as bisexual and currently know of none who are transgender individuals. (I very much hope that this statement will be out-of-date by the time the essay is published.)

Of course, I would like to see that multidimensional diversity among non-LGBTQ college and university presidents, and with more than four thousand institutions of higher education of every sort in the United States, we have both a long way to go and many opportunities. To have the pool of experienced administrators within higher education and allied sectors that we will need for this will require the professorial and administrative ranks to become much more diverse than they are. And there is every reason for us to want to see this achieved, because only when our pools are truly diverse at every step along the career path will we be sure that they can bring us the full measure of intellectual and inspirational potential that we need in higher education leadership.

We also need that diverse leadership for the sake of the diversity of the students who populate our campuses today and will in the coming years. Looked at nationally, our school system is so far from offering equal educational opportunities for all that one wonders if that is even a goal our fellow citizens share. (One could easily consider inequality of educational opportunity the greatest of our national shames were it not for the fact that there are so many other examples of glaring inequities.) Nonetheless, a fully diverse higher education leadership can be expected to make the greatest achievable impact on righting that wrong and broadening access and student success for all.

To bring these changes about, those who make governance decisions, in particular selection committees and governing bodies who appoint presidents—boards of trustees, regents, governors—will have to be persuaded. Nor should one forget national higher education organizations that are at once representative and influential (for example, the American Council on Education, the Association of American Universities, the American Association of State Colleges and Universities, the Association of Public and Land-Grant Universities, and the Association of Governing Boards). That both governing bodies and sector-wide national organizations should themselves be more diverse is axiomatic. What sitting LGBTQ presidents can do, of course, is model the special attributes we bring to our current leadership positions. Many of the authors in this volume have examined queer leadership as a special and significant factor in and of itself. I believe that whatever particular power leadership by self-identifying LGBTQ individuals has derives primarily from the strength and integrity that we needed to negotiate the hurdles and challenges that our identities and/or identifications present us in the world today. In addition, many of us have developed that kind of binocular vision that members of most minorities develop, that is, knowing that the view that is presented as "the norm" is not the only perspective, which in turn greatly increases the likelihood that we will be just that more empathetic toward other perspectives.

I am hopeful that despite the asymmetrical empowerment that too often characterized the gay movement through the twentieth century, it can contribute not just to diversity but to those indispensable further dimensions of equity and inclusion in the twenty-first. The real basis of my optimism is the students whom I have come to know on the campuses I have been a part of. Their convictions and commitment will, I am confident, carry us forward, and nowhere more consequentially than in a dimension of diversity not yet fully realized within our set of college and university presidents. As I noted above, to the extent we have a reliable census of LGBTQ college and university presidents, most represent the first two letters in that series. The next generation of leadership will by no means be so delimited. Going forward, making sure our institutions and the pathways toward leadership are fully inclusive, among these and all other imaginable and not-yet-imagined dimensions, is absolutely essential. All of us who have achieved leadership positions must support the next generation of ever more diverse leaders in their presidencies, in a world that has never been hospitable and that in some ways shows signs of becoming more volatile and hostile every day.

Now what can we as a group bring to that world to repair it, in the best spirit of and for the sake of a higher education worthy of that name? Specifically, I want to instance the rejection of gender binarism because it is among the newer concepts in this realm and one that students as much as faculty have helped me learn about, repairing my own ignorance, over the last twenty or so years. And, strange as it may at first seem, it is actually the learning I most want to point to, not the performativity of gender or any or all the insights that have been derived from it.

For however much it is an oft-quoted truism, it is deeply true that the discovery of knowledge and the deepening of understanding are the hallmarks of higher education. While many in our society readily acknowledge the new discoveries of the physical sciences—a gene, a galaxy, a subatomic particle, for example— few are inclined to acknowledge them in other realms. In my view, the discovery and growing awareness of nonbinarism in gender, replacing the male-female dichotomy that shaped (and limited) our vision of the world before, is as earthshaking a discovery as any in the natural sciences, whether heliocentrism, gravity, relativity, or the double helix of polynucleotide chains that is DNA.

Incubating such new discoveries is the essence of our colleges' and universities' missions, a process that involves, variously, the idea's first elaboration, its refinement through informed inquiry and structured debate, further elaboration, and a thinking-through of the impact that the new way of seeing will have in the world.

Over the past twenty to twenty-five years, LGBTQ individuals have thought that they could both be public about their self-identification and serve as college and university presidents. More and more institutions have selected such individuals, for their skills and fit for the job, of course, but no longer excluding them simply because they were gay- or lesbian-identified and honest about that fact. And gradually, hiring bodies, too, are becoming aware of the particular capacities and qualities of queer leadership.

Today, higher-education communities, not unlike society at large but often at the forefront, are thinking through what it means to move beyond the dichotomized approach to gender to a space that supports gender nonconformity. The assumption of college presidencies by LGBTQ individuals has itself already made an immense contribution to higher education, not merely in terms of demographic diversity—as important as that is—but also in expanding the conceivable, of changing minds and the way people think. It has helped us free ourselves from the assumptions of a previous era.

Some of higher education's critics on the right will associate the expansion of diversity to include sexual orientation and, what seems most currently of concern to them, gender identity and expression, as further examples of the "political correctness" that they believe infects and infests higher education. This is not the place to take on the rhetorical bad faith of those who target "PC." Put simply, I see the matter entirely differently. Granted, there may be some who adopt a given viewpoint without sufficient appreciation of its intellectual underpinnings, and that is an opportunity for college and universities to emphasize that we most fully represent higher education when we are prepared to interrogate seriously any and all orthodoxies, whether old or new, and demand to under-stand "why" and "in what way" (among a host of many possible questions in the brave spaces of our campuses). In reality, the con-cept of gender nonbinarism, stimulates critical thinking and in doing so promotes the proper work of colleges and universities pre-cisely because it itself challenges so many broadly accepted no-tions. Coming to understand it as a more advanced way of looking at the world itself models how higher education uses critical think-ing to establish deeper and more solid truths.

For me, then, a college presidency diversifying along ever more dimensions exemplifies and advances the truest mission of higher education. Embodying and asserting that mission is never more important than now, when so many members of our society mistake the point and value of higher education itself.

One final observation on the "world" in which we find our-selves. Let us never forget that for all our struggles, including seri-ous threats of physical violence and risk of death faced dispropor-tionately by some members of our community, the trans community especially and BIPOC more generally, we in North America, along with our colleagues in parts of Europe and a few other countries, live relatively privileged existences, even in the midst of a pandemic. Just as there have been certain sectors within US higher education in which we have only recently begun to see LGBTQ presidential representation—not to mention those in which to say that it will be a long time coming is an understatement, such as Roman Cath-olic and some other denominational institutions—so the battle for LGBTQ rights in many parts of the world is at a point where it would be unthinkable for someone publicly known to be gay or les-bian to be a college or university president. In many places, it is not simply LGBTQ rights that are at stake, but *all* LGBTQ lives.

In the future I envision, the degree to which we can diversify the college and university presidency, and celebrate not only that grow-ing diversification but the appreciation of the special positive attributes of queer leadership it at once represents and furthers, will help inspire positive change in other countries. The position of college or university president is highly respected virtually worldwide. It is my hope that groups larger than our own would hold will look at the rich diversity of presidential leadership in North American higher education as a positive expression of a society that values diversity along dimensions both visible and invisible and worthy of emulation for that very reason.

This will not be an easy engagement, but that is no reason not to engage globally. To be sure, there is considerable work to be done in every state and on every campus in the United States, and we should take on the work to advance diversity, equity, inclusion, and justice at home. But we should not fail to cast our view across the entire world. Consider the United Nation's Sustainable Development Goals, of which there are seventeen. Despite the political pressure against it from many quarters, the sixteenth, titled "Peace, Justice, and Strong Institutions," asserts that "People everywhere need to be free of fear from all forms of violence and feel safe as they go about their lives whatever their ethnicity, faith or sexual orientation." The list is not as long as the nondiscrimination lists on our campuses, and, the fifth goal, on "Gender Equality," seems not to have moved beyond the male-female binary in its singular focus on the empowerment of "women and girls." And yet, who could not support every one of the urgent recommendations under this rubric—for access to education, for freedom from mutilation and sexual violence, against child marriage—as first steps? It is our obligation to see that ending persecution of the nonbinary is added to the list at the earliest possible date.

College and university presidents lead and inspire, and we must not let our relative privilege pursuing excellence at US and Canadian institutions blind us to the responsibilities and opportunities that we have to do what we can to support those who, with bravery and at great personal risk, are seeking to initiate change in the hostile environments in which they find themselves. This, too, is an element of the future I see.

REFERENCE

Schulman, S. 2021. *Let the Record Show: A Political History of ACT UP New York, 1987–1993*. New York: Farrar, Straus and Giroux.

Contributors

Terry L. Allison is a professor of English at Indiana University South Bend, where he served as chancellor from 2013 to 2018. He received his AB in economics and political science and a master's degree in library and information science from the University of California, Berkeley, and a master's in comparative literature and a PhD in literature from University of California, San Diego. Before coming to IU South Bend, Allison was chair or co-chair of the Women's Studies program at California State University, San Marcos; dean of the College of Arts and Letters at California State University, Los Angeles; and provost at Governors State University. He served as co-chair of the Program Planning Committee, secretary/treasurer, and now serves as executive director of LGBTQ Presidents in Higher Education. Allison has authored works in several fields, including literature, film, and theater. His most recent works include a book of poetry, *CSU Haiku*, and a book chapter about a queer aquatic spectacle known as "The Pink Flamingo," and he is currently writing several plays. He has been awarded multiple government and foundation grants and was a Fulbright Administrative Fellow to the Republic of Korea.

Peggy Apple is a professor of early childhood education at Clarion University of Pennsylvania. She teaches undergraduate and graduate early childhood courses that focus on standards-based, constructivist curriculum approaches for young children. She holds a PhD in curriculum and instruction with a concentration in early childhood with a minor in education policy studies from Indiana University Bloomington. As a university faculty member for over thirty years, Apple has worked in Texas, Indiana, and Pennsylvania in various faculty and administrative roles. During her career she also served as a presidential/chancellor spouse for eight years—she is the wife of Karen Whitney. Before coming to Clarion University, she held a joint position as education program chair at Ivy Tech Community College and Indiana University with responsibility for transfer programs. Additionally, she taught at Indiana University Bloomington and at San Antonio College, where she ended her tenure as Early Childhood Education department chair. She regularly presents at national, state, and local events. Her publications and research focus on early childhood program quality and the leader's role in curriculum and quality improvement. Apple earned a bachelor of science degree from Ball State University in elementary education with an early childhood and kindergarten endorsement, and a master of education degree from Bank Street College of Education.

Nancy "Rusty" Barceló is nationally known for her work on equity and inclusion. She has served as president of Northern New Mexico College, interim vice president at Central Connecticut State University, visiting special assistant to the chancellor at University of Illinois at Urbana-Champaign, vice president / vice provost for Equity & Diversity at University of Minnesota and vice president / vice provost for Minority Affairs & Diversity at the University of Washington. Dr. Barceló held various positions at the University of Iowa from 1975 to 1996, focusing on diversity in academic and student affairs. She has received many awards, including the National Association of Chicanas & Chicano Studies 2012 Scholar Award and the New Mexico Hispano Round Table "Walk the Talk" Award, and she was named a Distinguished Alumnus of the University of Iowa and Distinguished Alumnus of the School of Behavioral Science at California State University, Chico. Dr. Barceló has taught as a professor in the College of Education at Northern New Mexico University, affiliate faculty in educational policy and administration at Graduate School University of Minnesota, and affiliate assistant professor at the American ethnic studies program of the University of Washington. She has offered various leadership courses and taught The College Experience: La Chicana y Las Mujeres. She has also taught several freshmen seminars, including Complexities and Dynamics of Identity in a Multicultural World.

Raymond E. Crossman is a social justice activist and educator. He was trained as a psychologist and family therapist and, since 1992, has served as faculty in clinical psychology. He is currently the longest-serving LGBTQ university president in North America. He was appointed president of Adler University in 2003, and during his tenure, the institution has grown from a graduate psychology school enrolling about 200 students to a university dedicated to advancing social justice—enrolling more than 1,800 students at its Chicago, Vancouver, and online campuses. He co-founded LGBTQ Presidents in Higher Education in 2010 and co-chaired the organization from 2015 to 2018. In 2015, he chaired the first national conference for development of LGBTQ leaders in higher education. In 2017, he became the first university president to publicly disclose his HIV status, and he has used his personal story to advocate for marginalized communities. He received his BS (summa cum laude) in psychology and fine arts from Fordham University; he earned his MA and PhD in clinical psychology from Temple University; and he studied at Philadelphia Child Guidance Clinic.

Erika Endrijonas currently serves as superintendent-president of Pasadena City College, a three-time Aspen Prize Top Ten College in Pasadena, California. She previously served as president of Los Angeles Valley College in the Los Angeles Community College District, as executive vice president at Oxnard College in the Ventura County Community College District, and as career and technical dean at Santa Barbara City College. Dr. Endrijonas is currently chair of the California Community College Athletic Association Board and co-chair of the LGBTQ Presidents in

Higher Education. She is a founding member of the Community College League of California LGBTQ Caucus. She teaches in the community college doctoral programs at both California State University, Northridge (CSUN) and California State University, Los Angeles. Dr. Endrijonas earned her bachelor's degree (magna cum laude) in history at CSUN and her master's degree and PhD in American and women's history at the University of Southern California, where she also earned a graduate certificate in the Study of Women and Men in Society. Her dissertation was a cultural history of American cookbooks published between 1945 and 1960, examining how cookbooks served as prescriptive literature for women and men in the home in the post–World War II years.

James Gandre has been president of Manhattan School of Music (an international conservatory in New York City with 1,000 students from more than 50 countries and nearly every state) since 2013. Previously, he was dean of Chicago College of Performing Arts (2000–2007), interim dean of the College of Education (2006–2007), and provost/executive vice president (2007–2013), all at Roosevelt University. As a performer, Jim has appeared as a tenor soloist with the Cleveland Orchestra, Philharmonia Baroque Orchestra, and members of the San Francisco Symphony, as well as at the Pepsico Summerfare with the London Classical Players. His professional choral engagements include more than 175 performances with the New York and Israel Philharmonics, Aix-en-Provence Festival (France) / Warsaw Symphony, the Metropolitan Opera and Royal Concertgebouw orchestras, and the San Francisco Symphony, as well as more than 20 commercial recordings and national television appearances including *The Today Show, Live from Lincoln Center*, and *The Pet Shop Boys*. In these performances, he has worked under such conductors as Leonard Bernstein, Zubin Mehta, Sir Colin Davis, Mstislav Rostropovich, Riccardo Chailly, Edo de Waart, Christopher Hogwood, and Roger Norrington. A Wisconsin native, he earned his BMus from Lawrence University, an MMus from San Francisco Conservatory of Music, and his EdD from the University of Nebraska–Lincoln.

Richard J. Helldobler is president of William Paterson University in Wayne, New Jersey, one of the state's largest public universities, with more than 10,000 students. He is the first openly gay public university president in both New Jersey and Illinois, where he previously served as interim president of Northeastern Illinois University in Chicago. Since joining William Paterson in 2018, he has opened a new residence hall; acquired new academic space; launched WP Online; and successfully relaunched its first-year program, developing comprehensive services to support student success. A first-generation student of immigrant heritage, his personal experience informs his goal of serving students for whom education is a means of social mobility. In nearly two decades of increasingly senior academic roles at California University of Pennsylvania, he was also the founding artistic director for *CalRep* Pennsylvania and the Mon Valley Ballet Theatre. He was a 2005–2006 American Council on Education Fellow and currently serves on the board of the American Association of State Colleges and Universities. He earned his PhD in theater and MA in speech and theater from Bowling Green State University, and a bachelor of business administration degree in marketing from the University of Toledo.

Susan E. Henking is a passionate leader in liberal education who persists in the belief that education can change the world despite its historic and ongoing flaws. As scholar, teacher, and administrator at the intersection of liberal education, religious studies, and LGBTQ studies, she coedited an early anthology titled *Que(e)rying Religion* (with Gary David Comstock, 1997), taught the first course on LGBTQ studies and religious studies in American higher education, and was recognized by the Association of American Colleges and Universities for a course on AIDS/HIV cocreated with a chemist. She is cofounder of an early major in LGBT studies at Hobart and William Smith Colleges, cofounder of a section of the American Academy of Religion focused on lesbian feminism and has worked to enhance the place of women leaders in higher education through her work with HERS. President emerita of Shimer College, Susan led Shimer from 2012 to 2017 as its first female (and only lesbian) president since its mid-nineteenth-century founder. Susan served as interim president of Salem Academy and College in Winston Salem, NC, during the 2020–2021 academic year. Susan received her BA in religious studies and sociology from Duke University and her MA/PhD from the University of Chicago in religion and psychological studies. She lives with her partner, Betty Bayer, an internationally recognized professor of women's studies, in zoomlandia and in the Finger Lakes region of New York.

Ralph J. Hexter was president of Hampshire College in Amherst, Massachusetts, from 2005 to 2010; his selection as an out gay man was reported nationally. He was actively involved in the establishment of LGBTQ Presidents in Higher Education. Following his presidency, he returned to the University of California—he had previously been a dean at UC Berkeley—to serve as provost and executive vice chancellor (2011–2020), and for a time, interim chancellor of UC Davis. Hexter has been engaged with LGBTQ issues since college, including as president of Harvard University's first undergraduate gay group his senior year. At Yale University he was actively involved in the founding of its Lesbian and Gay Studies Center. A scholar of classical Greek and Roman literatures among other literary traditions, he has published on the history of sexuality and assisted other scholars, most notably the late John Boswell. Hexter was featured in Kirk Snyder's *The G Quotient* (2006). He served on the UC President's Advisory Council on LGBT Students, Faculty, and Staff. He received the University of Massachusetts's Continuing the Legacy of Stonewall Award (2008) and the UC Davis Chancellor's Achievement Award for Diversity and Community (2019). He was elected a member of the American Academy of Arts and Sciences in 2016.

Theodora J. Kalikow grew up in Swampscott, Massachusetts. She graduated from Wellesley College with a BA in chemistry and holds master's and doctoral degrees in philosophy and history of science from MIT and Boston University. She taught for many years at the University of Massachusetts Dartmouth, serving there as professor of philosophy, department chair, and assistant to the president. She also led the faculty union. Her later career as a college and university administrator took her to Colorado, New Hampshire, and Maine. Theo served for eighteen years as president of the University of Maine Farmington, during which time UMF gained national recognition as a public liberal arts college, part of the Council of Public Liberal Arts Colleges (COPLAC). Theo is a co-founder of LGBTQ Presidents in Higher Education and chaired the group for a couple of years early in its existence. Since her alleged retirement she has served for the past several years as a mentor for the American Council on Education Fellows Program. Kalikow has served as interim president at the University of Southern Maine and has had two interim VPAA assignments in California and Colorado. She is a member of the Maine Women's Hall of Fame.

Daniel López, Jr. is a proud alumnus and current president at Harold Washington College, one of the City Colleges of Chicago. He has more than 25 years of administrative and teaching experience at diverse higher education institutions in Illinois. Dr. López is an immigrant, nonnative speaker, first-generation college student, and former undocumented student. His personal story of struggle, perseverance, and resilience as a Latinx and queer educator motivate him to continue to empower marginalized communities to become social justice advocates. A scholar of higher education administration, his research focuses on issues of Latinx leaders as agents of change transforming and shaping colleges and universities in support of access and opportunities for all. A tireless advocate for postsecondary higher education, he currently serves as the board president for the Illinois Latino Council on Higher Education and board member of Diversifying Faculty in Illinois. He received his AA in liberal arts from Harold Washington College, a BA in communications from the University of Illinois at Springfield, a MEd from Loyola University Chicago, and a PhD in higher education administration from Illinois State University.

Charles R. "Chuck" Middleton, after a six-decade career in both public and private institutions of higher education, retired as Roosevelt

University's fifth president in 2015. Subsequently he served as chairman of the board of trustees of the City Colleges of Chicago. Chuck is a senior consultant at the Association of Governing Boards and serves as a mentor to the American Council on Education Fellows Program. A British historian, in recognition of his academic achievements, he was elected a fellow of the Royal Historical Society in 1989. In addition to his passion for and work in higher education, Chuck has always been active in civic and community engagement. His service encompassed advocacy for inclusiveness and social justice for all people, with a personal focus on the LGBTQ community. Over the years he has served on numerous boards of nonprofit organizations including those of the American Council on Education, SAGE USA, and PFLAG National. The first publicly acknowledged out gay male president at the time of his Roosevelt appointment in 2002, Chuck was a founding member of the LGBTQ Presidents in Higher Education in 2010. After his retirement he served as its executive director, pro bono, until 2019.

DeRionne Pollard is currently the president of Nevada State College. When she wrote her essay for this volume, she was the president of Montgomery College, one of the largest undergraduate institutions in the state of Maryland, where she served for ten years. Dr. Pollard is deeply connected to her community, serving on the American Association of Community Colleges' Twenty-First Century Commission on the Future of Community Colleges and the Commission on Academic, Student, and Community Development. Dr. Pollard is a member of the Equity Advisory Board for Mission Partners and the Center for First-Generation Student Success Advisory Board for the National Association of Student Personnel Administrators. Dr. Pollard was named one of Washington's 100 Most Powerful Women by *Washingtonian* Magazine, won a 2017 Academic Leadership Award from the Carnegie Corporation of New York and a Visionary Award from the Washington Area Women's Foundation. She holds a BA and an MA in English from Iowa State University, and a PhD in educational leadership and policy studies in higher education from Loyola University Chicago.

Katherine Hancock Ragsdale, an Episcopal priest, is the emerita president, dean, and professor of Applied Theology of Episcopal Divinity School, a graduate school of theological education formerly in Cambridge, MA, where she served from 2009 to 2015. Ragsdale was the second woman president of an Episcopal seminary in the United States (third in the worldwide Anglican Communion) and the first and only out president of an accredited graduate school of theological education in the United States. She was a founding co-chair of LGBTQ Presidents in Higher Education. A lifelong lesbian feminist activist, Ragsdale is the former president and CEO of the National Abortion Federation (NAF), the NAF Hotline, and NAF Canada. Ragsdale holds an AB from the College of William and Mary, an MDiv from Virginia Theological Seminary, and a DMin from Episcopal Divinity School.

Regina Stanback Stroud is an antiracist activist and committed practitioner facilitating diversity, equity and inclusion literacy development. She dedicated 35 years of her life's work to being a higher education leader and educator—including service as the chancellor of Peralta Community College District and the president of Skyline College. She is now the CEO of RSS Consulting, LLC. Dr. Stanback Stroud served President Barack Obama on his President's Advisory Council on Financial Capability for Young Americans. Her work in equity and leadership is recognized by the Academic Senate for California Community Colleges' statewide Regina Stanback Stroud Diversity Award and the Western Regional Council on Black American Affairs' Dr. Regina Stanback Stroud Leadership Achievement Award, both awarded to individuals committed to leadership excellence, equity, and social justice. Dr. Stanback Stroud holds a doctorate and master's degree in educational leadership from Mills College, a master's degree in human relations from Golden Gate University, and a bachelor of science in nursing sciences from Howard University. Dr. Stanback Stroud's scholarship and expertise have focused on student equity and diversity; education/industry collaboratives; economic empowerment and antipoverty strategies; community workforce and economic development; and regional and state educational policy.

Boris Thomas contributes to this volume in the partnership chapter and is the husband of James Gandre. Boris has been a psychotherapist in private practice for 20 years, first in Chicago, now in Manhattan, where he also is an executive coach. A former litigator, Boris practiced for ten years, specializing in labor and employment law. He is a retired member of the New York and New Jersey bars. Boris was a researcher at Chapin Hall Center for Children at the University of Chicago, where he worked on projects funded by the Pew Charitable Trusts and the Annie E. Casey Foundation, among others. He has a BA from Wesleyan University. He earned his MSW and JD from NYU, and his PhD from Chicago's Institute for Clinical Social Work, where he is on the faculty. He also has taught at DePaul University (Chicago) and the Institute for Contemporary Psychotherapy (New York). Boris was trained in the Columbia Coaching Certification Program, a joint program of Columbia University Business School and Teachers College. Boris's clinical authorship and presentations focus on trauma, race, and intersectionality. Supporting his clinical work with trauma, he is an EMDR practitioner, certified by the EMDR International Association.

Karen Whitney has held a variety of executive and leadership positions with increasing levels of responsibility, currently serving as the interim chancellor at the University of Illinois at Springfield and previously served as interim chancellor for the Pennsylvania Association of State System of Higher Education, president of Clarion University, and vice chancellor for student life at Indiana University–Purdue University Indianapolis as well as holding a variety of leadership positions at the University of Texas at San Antonio and the University of Houston. Karen is a nationally recognized organizational and leadership development writer, speaker, consultant, and advisor. She holds a doctorate from the University of Texas at Austin in higher education administration and is a certified coach through the Center for Executive Coaching. Karen is passionately focused on working with leaders and executives to ensure their success in service to their students and institutions. In working with every leader to succeed, Karen's approach is to combine a proven track-record of higher education leadership with a variety of engagement approaches, including advising, coaching, facilitating, and training. Drawing on her vast experience at every level of leadership, she customizes an individual structured process to ensure each leader achieves their highest professional and institutional priorities.

Index

fit-filter, 141, 146–47, 151
Foote, Brangwyn, 107
Frank, Barney, 161
Friedman, Edwin, 124

Gandre, James: on becoming an LGBTQ president or leader, 145, 150–53; on coming out and being out, 49, 54–57; on partner's role, 131, 136–39; on self-care, 119–22
gay marriage, 14–15, 64, 88, 109, 134. *See also* partners of presidents
"Gay Men Need to Be Feminists, Too" (Benjamin), 26
Gay Pride parades, 3, 98
Gay Student Services v. Texas A&M University (1984), 98
gender: homophobia and, 94, 97; identity and, 8–9; inclusion and, 67, 69; intersectionality and, 35, 38; mentorship and, 115–16; nonbinarism, 165–67
gender-neutral restrooms, 69–70, 94
gender roles: feminist leadership and, 26–27, 31; heteronormativity and, 83; partners of presidents and, 141–42
Gonzalez, Alexander, 115

Hampshire College, 52–53, 132–34
Helldobler, Richard J.: on leading in heteronormative world, 77, 82–85; on mentorship, 105, 109–12
Henking, Susan, 91, 101–4
Henley, Jean, 106
heteronormativity: Crossman on, 77–81; Helldobler on, 77, 82–85; identity and, 9–10; internalization of, 18, 80, 88, 119; Kalikow on, 77, 86–89; leader-navigator approach and, 12–15; leading in heteronormative world, 77–89; mentoring and, 110; privilege and, 58; recruitment and search processes and, 82–85; sports references as markers of, 78–79
Hexter, Ralph J.: on coming out and being out, 49, 50–53; on future of

LGBTQ presidency and leadership, 160–69; on partner's role, 131–35
high school experiences, 27, 86–87, 97
HIV/AIDS, 16, 18, 40–43, 161–62
hobbies, 127
Hollander, Gary, 5
homophobia: Allison on, 91–96; feminist leadership and, 21–22, 31; Henking on, 91, 101–4; heteronormativity and, 79–80; inclusion and, 70; institutionalized, 92; leading in a homophobic world, 91–104; Whitney on, 91, 97–100
The Homosexual Agenda (film), 93
Houston GLBT Political Caucus, 97
How Will You Measure Your Life? (Christensen), 156
Hrabowski, Freeman A., III, 137
hyper-focus, 123

identity, 7–19; affirmation of, 46–47, 59–60; coming out and, 57; Crossman on, 7, 16–19; culture of institution and, 148; Endrijonas on, 7–11; homophobia and, 102–3; inclusion and, 68, 71, 74; intersectionality and, 2, 12, 35–36, 38, 40–41, 44–47; leader-navigator, 12–15; sexual, 38, 84–85, 93, 111, 115; Whitney on, 7, 12–15. *See also* gender
immigrants: self-care and, 125; undocumented, 72
imposter syndrome, 119
inclusion on campus, 63–75; Endrijonas on, 63, 68–71; heterosexism and, 78–79; López on, 63, 72–75; multiculturalism and, 92–93; Stanback Stroud on, 63–67
Indiana University South Bend, 29, 93–96
intersectionality, 35–47; Barceló on, 35, 44–47; class and, 35, 38; Crossman on, 35, 40–43; marginalization and, 45–46; Pollard on, 35–39

Jensen, Robert, 26
Jones, Barbara, 106
Journal of Homosexuality, 26

Kalikow, Theodora J., 2; on leading in heteronormative world, 77, 86–89; on mentorship, 105–8; on self-care, 119, 128–30
kickboxing, 126–27
Kinsey Institute, 94
Krasny, Michael, 65
Kushner, Tony, 18

Latinx community: future of LGBTQ leadership and, 163; inclusion initiatives and, 72, 74; mentorship and, 115
leadership: becoming an LGBTQ president or leader, 145–58; coming out and, 49–61; dancing and, 42–43; feminist, 21–34; future of, 160–69; gender and, 8–9; in heteronormative world, 77–89; in homophobic world, 91–104; of inclusion on campus, 63–75; intersectionality and, 35–47; leader-navigator style, 12–15; LGBTQ identity and, 7–19; mentorship and, 105–17; partners of presidents and, 131–43; self-care and, 119–30
LGBTQ Presidents in Higher Education, 3–4, 8, 53, 108, 113, 162
life cycle of presidency. See presidential life cycle
López, Daniel, Jr., 63, 72–75

male privilege, 22–23, 24, 82
Manhattan School of Music, 3, 56, 57, 122, 136, 152
marginalization: coming out and, 58; inclusion and, 72; intersectionality and, 45–46; language of, 66; self-care and, 123
Marks, Jeanette, 2
Marx, Groucho, 92, 94
Mattfeld, Jacquelyn A., 2
McRobbie, Michael, 94
meditation, 126
mentorship, 105–17; Allison on, 105, 113–17; Helldobler on, 105, 109–12; Kalikow on, 105–8
microaggressions, 44

Middleton, Charles R. "Chuck," 2–3, 111–12, 152
Milk, Harvey, 54, 55, 97–98, 161
misogyny: feminist leadership and, 21–22, 26–28, 32; homophobia as subset of, 24, 102; inclusion and, 70
Montgomery College, 36–39
Moral Majority, 97
Mount Holyoke College, 2
multiculturalism, 92–93

National Association for College Admission Counseling, 56
National Coming Out Day, 50
National Identification Program (ACE), 107
neuroplasticity, 127
Noble, Elaine, 161
non-anxious presence, 124
nonbinarism, 165–67

oppression: coming out and, 58; feminist leadership and, 25; heteronormativity and, 77; identity and, 17–18; inclusion and, 63; intersectionality and, 40–42, 44, 46; structural, 101
Ouellette, Bill, 5
out-boarding process, 149

partners of presidents, 131–43; Gandre and Thomas on, 131, 136–39; Hexter on, 131–35; Whitney and Apple on, 131, 140–43
patriarchy: feminism and, 22, 24, 28; homophobia and, 22; identity and, 13; mentorship and, 116
Pence, Mike, 94
Pennsylvania State System of Higher Education, 145–46
Phelps, Fred, 24
Pollard, DeRionne, 35–39
Portraits of Life: LBGT Stories of Being (photography exhibition), 39
presidential leadership. See leadership
presidential life cycle, 140–43, 145; acquiring stage, 141–42, 147–48; adjourning stage, 143, 148–49;

aspiring stage, 140–41, 146–47; attending stage, 142–43, 148

privilege: coming out and, 50, 59; feminist leadership and, 24–25; heteronormativity and, 82; homophobia and, 95; identity and, 8, 10, 13, 17; inclusion and, 64–65, 70–72; intersectionality and, 42, 45; male, 22–23, 24, 82; white, 21, 24–25, 33, 41, 82

Que(e)rying Religion: A Critical Anthology (eds. Henking and Comstock), 102

race: feminist leadership and, 28, 31; inclusion and, 67; intersectionality and, 38; mentorship and, 115; self-care and, 125

Ragsdale, Katherine Hancock: on becoming an LGBTQ president or leader, 145, 154–58; on feminist leadership, 21–25; on self-care, 119, 123–27

Real Queer America: LGBTQ Stories from Red States (Allen), 94

recruitment processes for university leadership, 82–85, 140–42, 151–52

Regina Stanback Stroud Diversity Award, 66

religion: faith-based institutions, 93; homophobia and, 93, 102; intersectionality and, 38; self-care and, 126

Religious Freedom Restoration Act (Indiana), 94–95

Renn, Kristen, 113

restorative justice, 104

restrooms, gender-neutral and single-use, 69–70, 94

Rich, Adrienne: "Compulsory Heterosexuality and Lesbian Existence," 102

Robinson, Bryan E.: *Chained to the Desk: A Guidebook for Workaholics, Their Partners and Children, and the Clinicians Who Treat Them*, 121

Roosevelt University, 3, 57, 111, 152

Same-Sex Unions (Boswell), 51

Schmidt, Benno, 133

search processes for university leadership, 82–85, 140–42, 151–52

self-care, 119–30; Gandre on, 119–22; Kalikow on, 119, 128–30; Ragsdale on, 119, 123–27

Senter, Ash, 5

sexism. *See* misogyny

sexuality and sexual orientation: feminist leadership and, 27, 32; future of LGBTQ leadership and, 167, 169; heteronormativity and, 77–89; homophobia and, 91–104; identity and, 7–10; inclusion and, 64, 67, 68–69, 72, 74; intersectionality and, 38; mentorship and, 110

Shimer College, 103

single-use restrooms, 69–70, 94

sleep, 127, 128

social justice, 9, 11, 41, 53, 64–66

social media, 50, 97, 109–10

Sondheim, Stephen, 112

Southeastern Massachusetts University, 106

sports references, 78–79, 135

Stanback Stroud, Regina: on coming out, 49, 58–61; on inclusion on campus, 63–67; "Leading to Transgress" leadership framework, 64–65

standpoint theory, 22

Stonewall Riots, 159

stress: partners of presidents and, 137; self-care and, 123–25

Supreme Court on LGBTQ rights, 98

Sustainable Development Goals (UN), 168

Teeter, Lura Shaffner, 106

temperament, 51, 154, 156–57

Thomas, Boris, 131, 136–39

undocumented immigrants, 72

United Nations Sustainable Development Goals, 168

University of California, Berkeley, 27, 52